C000120504

CliffsNotes
Making
Windows® 98
Work for You

By Brian Underdahl

IN THIS BOOK

- Getting started with Windows
- Connecting to the Internet
- Organizing your projects
- Customizing your computer
- Reinforce what you learn with CliffsNotes Review
- Find more Windows information in CliffsNotes Resource Center and online at www.cliffsnotes.com

IDG Books Worldwide, Inc.
An International Data Group Company

Foster City, CA • Chicago, IL • Indianapolis, IN • New York, NY

IDG
BOOKS
WORLDWIDE

About the Author

Brian Underdahl has written or contributed to more than 40 books about computing. Brian also writes for magazines about computers, teaches numerous computer classes, and speaks to professional organizations.

Publisher's Acknowledgments

Editorial

Senior Project Editor: Pat O'Brien
Acquisitions Editor: Andy Cummings
Copy Editor: Ted Cains
Technical Editors: Sally Neuman, Bob Correll
Editorial Assistant: Jamila Pree

Production

Indexer: York Production Services
Proofreader: York Production Services
IDG Books Indianapolis Production Department

 is a registered trademark or trademark under exclusive license to IDG Books Worldwide, Inc. from International Data Group, Inc. in the United States and/or other countries.

Table of Contents

INTRODUCTION

If you use a computer, the chances are pretty good that the computer uses Windows 98. If so, you're probably wondering just what this Windows 98 thing really is and why your PC needs it.

Windows 98 is an *operating system*, which simply means that Windows 98 is software that helps your computer function.

Why Do You Need This Book?

Can you answer yes to any of these questions?

- Do you need to learn about Windows fast?
- Don't have time to read 500 pages about your new computer?
- Want to access the Internet in record time?
- Want to customize your computer just right?

If so, then CliffsNotes *Making Windows 98 Work for You* is for you!

How to Use This Book

CliffsNotes *Making Windows 98 Work for You* is a fast introduction to the world of Windows 98, whether you're a first-time computer user or just new to Windows 98. I've organized the chapters in a logical progression so that you can do real things with your computer in short order. You can skip around from topic to topic if you want.

Experienced PC users can skim through the chapters and topics to learn what's new and different about Windows 98. The chapter introductions are brief and tell you whether the chapter is of particular interest to you.

Whether you're new or a veteran, you'll appreciate the icons that identify paragraphs of particular interest.

Think of these paragraphs as the essential truths you must remember.

Impress your friends and confound your enemies with these gems.

Be wary! You can create big problems if you ignore this advice.

Don't Miss Our Web Site

Keep up with the exciting world of computing by visiting the CliffsNotes Web site at www.cliffsnotes.com. Here's what you find:

■ Interactive tools that are fun and informative

■ Links to interesting Web sites

■ Additional resources to help you continue your learning

At www.cliffsnotes.com, you can even register for a new feature called CliffsNotes Daily, which offers you newsletters on a variety of topics, delivered right to your e-mail inbox each business day.

If you haven't yet discovered the Internet and are wondering how to get online, pick up *Getting On the Internet*, new from CliffsNotes. You'll learn just what you need to make your online connection quickly and easily. See you at www.cliffsnotes.com!

CHAPTER 1

CATCHING UP TO 98

IN THIS CHAPTER

- Defining Windows 98
- Starting Windows

Computers are really just electronic machines. They are very complex machines, but machines nonetheless. *Software* — instructions that tell the computer what to do — makes computers do useful things, such as help you write a letter, watch your stock portfolio, or view information on the Internet. Without these instructions, a computer can't do anything.

Software packages also are known as *applications* and *programs*.

Windows 98 is a kind of software program called an *operating system*. This special type of software enables your computer — your *hardware* — and your software to work together. Without an operating system, such as Windows 98, a computer doesn't know how to use applications.

Software is usually designed to run on computers that use a specific operating system. If your PC has Windows 98, then your programs should be designed for Windows 98. Be sure to look at the system requirements on the software package before you buy new software and make certain that the program runs on Windows 98 (or Windows 95 if Windows 98 is not specifically mentioned).

Starting Windows 98

Windows 98 should start automatically when you switch your PC on. The power switch may be on the front, side, or back of the PC cabinet. The monitor probably has a separate power switch — you need to switch it on, too.

When you first start up your PC, you probably have to wait a few moments while Windows 98 loads.

Eventually, you see the Windows 98 *desktop,* several program *icons,* and the Start button. You may also see an hourglass in the middle of your screen. After the hourglass disappears, your computer is ready for you to use.

Windows 98 provides you with a *graphical user interface*, or GUI (pronounced "gooey"), so that you can work with your computer by using on-screen icons and menus. This means that you can use your mouse and your keyboard to select the program or document that you want to use instead of trying to remember some esoteric command-line instruction. GUIs make computers far easier to use than they were in the days when you had to type commands to do anything — for one thing, you don't have to worry about typing in the wrong command. Figure 1-1 shows a typical Windows 98 screen.

The important Windows desktop features are covered in this book. Table 1-1 shows where to look in the book.

Table 1-1: Windows Desktop

Feature	Location
Start button	Chapter 2
Taskbar	Chapter 2
Taskbar button	Chapter 2
Recycle Bin	Chapter 5
System Tray	Chapter 6

Figure 1-1:　The Windows desktop is your entry point for the computer.

 Chapter 3 explains how to use your mouse and your keyboard.

What Else Is There?

 Windows 98 isn't the only operating system that's available for PCs. You've probably heard of some of them and may wonder how they compare to Windows 98. A few of the popular options include Linux, BeOS, and the Mac OS.

One thing that each of these alternatives share is that none of them is compatible with Windows 98. The Windows 98 application programs on your PC won't work on computers that use these other operating systems.

A couple of operating systems are fairly compatible with Windows 98. Windows 95 (the predecessor to Windows 98) is quite similar to Windows 98 and is still in use on lots of PCs. Windows NT 4 and its upcoming successor Windows 2000 are also similar to Windows 98. Most programs that run on Windows 98 also run on Windows NT 4 and Windows 2000. To run efficiently, both Windows NT 4 and Windows 2000 require more powerful PCs than is necessary for Windows 98.

CHAPTER 2
RUNNING PROGRAMS

IN THIS CHAPTER

- Defining programs
- Opening and starting programs
- Switching between programs
- Closing programs

If you want your PC to be something a bit more useful than a large gray paperweight, you have to run programs on the computer. In this chapter, you learn the essentials of running programs on your Windows 98 PC.

What Are Programs?

Programs — commonly known as *applications* — are the pieces of software that make your computer perform specific tasks. Computers are extremely adaptable tools that use programs to enable them to perform very specific functions. For example, here are some popular programs that you can use to make your Windows 98 PC do some very different things:

- *Microsoft Word, Corel WordPerfect,* and *Lotus WordPro* enable your PC to function as a word processor.

- *Microsoft Excel, Corel Quattro Pro,* and *Lotus 1-2-3* enable your PC to function as a highly advanced electronic spreadsheet.

- *Internet Explorer, Netscape Navigator,* and *Opera* enable your PC to function as a tool for navigating and viewing the millions of pages of information on the Internet.

■ *Microsoft Flight Simulator, Quake,* and *Myst* enable your PC to play games with exciting video and sounds.

Of course, these are just a few examples of the thousands of different programs that you can run on your PC.

In Windows 98, any work that you create is considered a *document.* Windows 98 remembers which program you used to create your documents, and it uses this information to enable you to open a document directly without first opening the appropriate application program — Windows 98 opens the correct program for you.

Automatically opening the correct program when you open a document saves you a few steps when you're working with existing documents, but you still need to open the appropriate program to create new documents. In the following sections, you see several different methods for doing so. You can choose the method that's most convenient for you.

Opening and Starting Programs

Programs are stored in files on the disk drives that are contained in your computer. To actually use a program, your computer must load the program from the disk drive into the computer's memory.

The method that you use to load a program into memory is up to you. Because Windows 98 is highly graphical, most of the methods involve pointing and clicking with your mouse, or selecting an item using your keyboard.

Starting with the Start button

The *Start button* appears in the lower-left corner of your Windows 98 desktop. The Start button leads to a pop-up

menu — the *Start menu* — that contains entries for many of
the programs that are installed on your PC. Figure 2-1 shows
how the Start menu appears when you click the Start button.

Figure 2-1:   Click the Start button to display the Start menu.

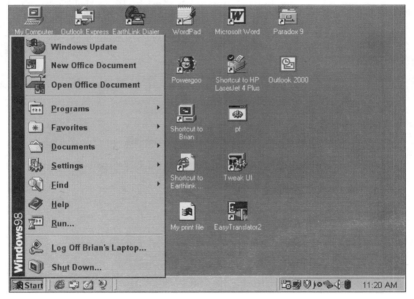

You can activate the Start button and display the Start menu
several different ways:

■ Move the mouse pointer over the Start button and click
the left mouse button once.

■ Hold down the Ctrl key and press the Esc key.

■ If your keyboard has a Windows key — a key with the
wavy Windows flag — press it.

Both keyboard methods work even if the Start button is hidden. If the taskbar is hidden, you can usually cause it to
appear by moving the mouse pointer just below the bottom

edge of the screen, and after the taskbar is visible, click the Start button. Sometimes, however, this doesn't work because the taskbar can be hidden at any edge of the screen, or another program may prevent it from popping up.

Notice that many items on the Start menu have a small right-pointing triangle to the right of the item. This triangle indicates that another menu appears when you move the mouse pointer over the item. Slide the mouse over the second menu and then over the name of the program you wish to run. When the correct program is highlighted, click the left mouse button once to run the program.

Starting with desktop icons

Your Windows 98 desktop contains a number of *icons* — small pictures that represent different programs and documents that are available on your PC. You can use these icons to open the associated programs or documents.

PCs can be configured to open items with either a single mouse click or with a double mouse click. Here's how to find out which method works on your computer. Move the mouse pointer over one of the icons on the desktop and click the left mouse button once. Watch what happens:

■ If the mouse pointer changes to an hourglass and the program or document opens, you can open items on the desktop using a single click.

■ If the mouse pointer does not change, the item does not open, and the name below the icon becomes highlighted, you must use a double-click to open items on the desktop. A *double-click* is two very quick clicks of the left mouse button in a row.

■ If nothing happens, move the mouse pointer slightly to make certain it's actually over the icon, and then try again. It's easy to place the pointer incorrectly at first. With practice, you'll get it.

You learn more about using the mouse and making it work the way you want in Chapter 3.

Starting with Windows Explorer

All the items you may want to open may not appear on the Start menu or on your desktop. There simply isn't room for everything to appear in the Start menu or desktop.

Windows Explorer enables you to locate and open items anywhere on your PC. Figure 2-2 shows Windows Explorer as it appears on a typical PC.

Figure 2-2:   Use Windows Explorer to locate and open items anywhere on your PC.

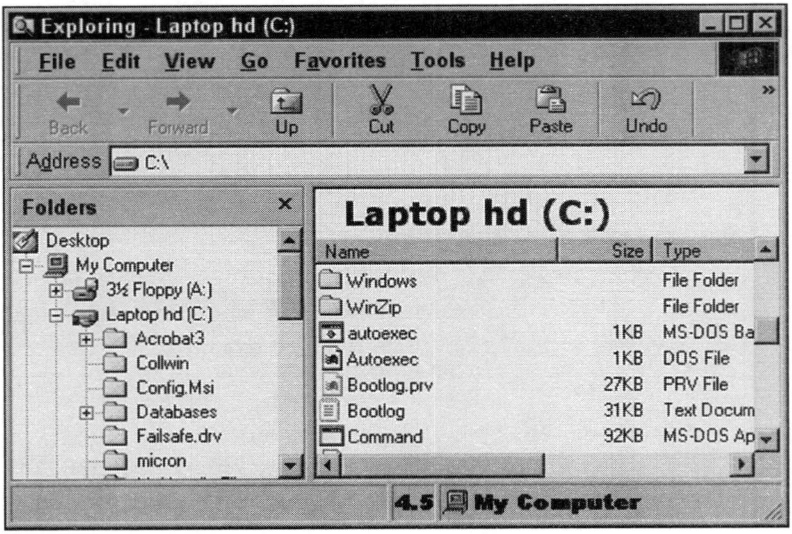

To open Windows Explorer, click the Start button to open the Start menu. Then move the pointer up to open the Programs menu and click Windows Explorer.

Finding and opening an item that appears in Windows Explorer takes a combination of techniques that are similar to those you use on the Start menu and your desktop. Opening Windows Explorer items requires the same number of mouse clicks as opening items on your desktop. If you have to double-click to open items on the desktop, you must also double-click to open items in Windows Explorer.

You learn more about using Windows Explorer in Chapter 4.

Starting with the Run dialog box

Although Windows 98 primarily uses pointing and clicking, you can still type out commands if necessary. You can do this one of two ways in Windows 98. The method you use depends on what you're trying to accomplish. If you simply want to start a program — such as an installation program on a CD-ROM — you can use the Run dialog box. This is a small box that appears when you click the Start button and then select Run.

Figure 2-3 shows an example of how you can use the Run dialog box to issue a command that runs Windows Explorer in a special way. In this case, the command is `explorer /e,/root,"c:\my documents"` This command tells Windows 98 to open Windows Explorer showing only the My Documents folder and anything contained in that folder.

You can also type certain commands at the MS-DOS Prompt, which you can find on the Programs menu. You probably don't want to use the MS-DOS Prompt unless you know what you're doing or are being assisted by someone else who knows.

Figure 2-3:   Use the Run dialog box to issue commands for running programs.

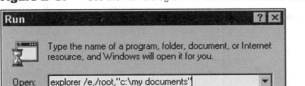

Switching between Programs

Modern PCs can run more than one program at the same time. You might load your e-mail program, your word processor, and a spreadsheet program at the same time. When you want to switch from one task to another, you can switch without closing the program you're using.

To run more than one program at the same time, simply use the Start menu, the desktop icons, Windows Explorer, or the Run dialog box to open each program. Then click the appropriate taskbar button to switch to a different program. Figure 2-4 shows how the Windows 98 taskbar appears when three different programs are running at the same time.

Figure 2-4:   Use the taskbar buttons to switch between open programs.

You can also switch between open programs using your keyboard. Hold down the Alt key and press the Tab key. This box shows icons for the programs that are currently open. While you hold down the Alt key, the highlight moves to the next program in the list each time you press the Tab key. When the program you want is selected, release the Alt key to switch to that program. You may find that using the

Alt+Tab key combination is a little easier than clicking the correct taskbar button — especially if you have a large number of programs loaded at the same time.

Closing Programs

When you're finished using a program, closing the program is a good idea. Closing programs you no longer need frees up memory so that your other programs can run a bit faster.

Most Windows 98 programs have an Exit command on their File menu (although some programs may label this command Close). If you click the File item on the program's menu bar, the File menu opens, and you can scroll down to select Exit.

If you haven't saved your work when you choose File⇨Exit, you'll probably see a message asking if you want to save your changes, discard those changes, or cancel and return to the program. Each program displays a slightly different message, but you should be careful not to ignore the message because you could lose any work you've done since you last saved the document.

In addition to the File⇨Exit command, Windows 98 programs also have a Close button in the upper-right corner of their program window. This button has the X in it. Clicking the Close button is the equivalent of selecting File⇨Exit or File⇨Close.

CHAPTER 3

TYPING, POINTING, AND CLICKING

IN THIS CHAPTER

- Pointing and clicking
- Mastering your keyboard

Someday, we may simply talk to our computers and they'll understand what we want them to do. Until then, you're pretty much stuck using the keyboard and mouse to interact with your PC. In this chapter, you learn how to do so as well as how you can adjust both of them to better suit your needs.

Pointing and Clicking

People who are unfamiliar with using a mouse often feel a little uncomfortable with the mouse at first, and this sometimes leads them to try to avoid using the mouse as much as possible. In a highly graphical environment like Windows 98, avoiding the mouse is difficult.

Even if moving the mouse around and clicking things seems awkward at first, you'll soon discover that your mouse and Windows 98 were made for each other.

Moving the pointer on the screen

When you move your mouse, the on-screen pointer moves along in the same direction. If you move the mouse forward, the pointer moves up on the screen. If you move the mouse to the right, the pointer also moves to the right. If the pointer does not move in the same direction as the mouse, make certain that you're holding the mouse so that the cord sticks out at the end that is the farthest from the edge of your desk and is in contact with the surface of your desk.

Some PCs use an alternate means of moving the pointer. Laptop PCs often use a touch pad or a small pointing stick (about the size of a pencil eraser that sticks up in the middle of the keyboard). Roller balls are another option for moving the pointer. Here is how you use these alternative pointing devices:

- Slide one finger across a touch pad in the direction that you want the pointer to move. Avoid allowing more than one finger to touch the pad — this confuses your system and may cause the pointer to jump erratically. Never use a pen or any other type of device on a touch pad! Also be careful not to tap on the touch pad because this is usually interpreted as clicking the left mouse button.

- Apply pressure to a pointing stick in the direction that you want the pointer to move. The pointing stick won't actually move, but it does sense the pressure that you apply and moves the pointer in the correct direction.

- Roll the roller ball in the direction that you want the pointer to move.

If your laptop PC has both a touch pad and a pointing stick, you'll probably find that only one of them can be active. Switching between the two is generally done by pressing certain key combinations. Refer to your user manual to find out exactly how to make the switch on your system.

If the mouse pointer seems to move erratically, you may need to clean the mouse or place it on a better surface.

■ The small ball in the bottom of the mouse usually is removable. Take out the ball and wash it with plain warm water.

■ A good mouse pad is a good investment. If possible, find a mouse pad with a surface texture like denim jeans — this generally provides the traction needed for smooth pointer movement.

Clicking the left mouse button

After you move the mouse pointer over an object on your desktop, the next step is actually doing something with the object. That's where the mouse buttons come into the picture. Unfortunately, that's also where a certain amount of confusion comes into the picture as well.

The problem is that sometimes you must click once, and sometimes you must *double-click* — which means you must quickly click the button twice in a row. To further complicate matters, different PCs may be configured to use a single click where others require a double-click to perform the same action.

Generally, though, you can safely assume certain things about mouse clicks:

■ A single click opens a menu or activates a command that appears on a program's menu. Menus never require a double-click.

■ If the names under desktop icons are underlined, a single click activates the object that is associated with the icon. You can tell that an icon has been activated if the pointer changes to an hourglass.

■ If the icon names are not underlined, a single click usually just selects the icon. In this case, you need to double-click to activate it.

■ Windows Explorer uses the same number of clicks as the desktop icons, so if you use a single click to activate desktop icons, you also use single clicks to open items in Windows Explorer.

You can change between the single- and double-click settings to see which style you prefer. Here's how:

1. Choose Start⇨Programs⇨Windows Explorer to open Windows Explorer.

2. Select View⇨Folder Options to open the Folder Options dialog box.

3. On the General tab, as shown in Figure 3-1, choose one of these options:

Choose *Web style* to activate objects with a single click.

Choose Classic style to activate objects using double-clicks.

4. Click OK.

Your changes take effect immediately, and you can make the change as often as you like.

Clicking the right mouse button

The PC mouse always has at least two buttons, and those buttons serve very different purposes. If you click the wrong button, you aren't likely to achieve the desired results.

By default, the left mouse button selects or activates items. When someone tells you to click or double-click an object, they usually mean that you should use the left button.

Figure 3-1:   The Folder Options dialog box.

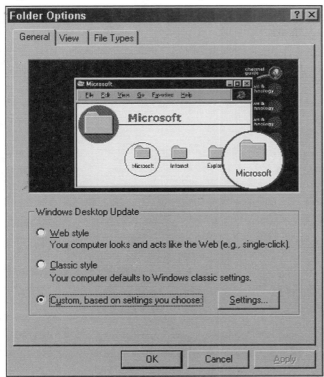

The right mouse button generally displays a *context sensitive menu* for an item, which means that the menu lists only actions that you can perform on the selected object. Right-click menus change according to the type of object you select.

Some mice have a third button or even a small wheel between the buttons. The function of the third button varies depending on the type of mouse and the application that you're using. The small wheel is typically used for *scrolling* — moving around on a page that is displayed on your screen.

Dragging and dropping

In Windows 98, you can use your mouse to easily copy or move objects by using a technique known as *drag and drop*. You select an object and then use your mouse to drag it to the desired destination. As you drag the object, you hold down the left mouse button and release it only when the mouse pointer is pointing to the location where you want to drop the object.

Here are some special techniques you can use with drag and drop:

■ To move an object to a new location on the same disk drive, select the object, hold down the left mouse button to drag it to a new location, and drop it by releasing the button.

■ To move an object to a new location on a different disk drive, hold down the Shift key while you drag and drop it.

■ To copy an object to a location on the same disk drive, select the object, hold down the Ctrl key while you hold down the left mouse button to drag it to a new location, and then drop it by releasing the button.

■ To copy an object to a location on a different disk drive, select the object, hold down the left mouse button to drag it to a new location, and drop it by releasing the button.

You can also drag and drop objects to and from most Windows 98 documents. You must, however, drop the object onto the correct application window — you can't drop objects onto the taskbar buttons. If you can't see the destination window, move the mouse pointer onto the taskbar button, continue to hold down the left mouse button, and then drag the object into the window when it opens.

If you want to drag and drop multiple items, select all the items before you begin to drag them to a new location. You can select multiple items two different ways:

■   To select a contiguous range of items, select the first item in the list, hold down the Shift key, and move the mouse pointer to select the final item. Those two items and all the items in between are highlighted.

■   To select items that are not adjacent, hold down the Ctrl key as you select each item. Select an item a second time to remove it from the selection.

Simplifying your mouse

If you find that using the left mouse button most of the time feels awkward, or that Windows 98 doesn't respond properly when you double-click, you can adjust the mouse settings to make using the mouse a bit easier. You can also adjust a number of other mouse settings.

To adjust your mouse settings, follow these steps:

1.   Choose Start➪Settings➪Control Panel. The Control Panel window appears.

2.   Click the Mouse icon to open the Mouse Properties dialog box (see Figure 3-2).

3.   To swap the functions of the right and left mouse buttons, choose the button configuration option that you prefer.

4.   To make the mouse respond to your double-clicks, drag the Double-click speed slider left or right and then double-click in the Test area box.

5.   Click the Motion tab to adjust the speed that the mouse pointer moves and whether you want a pointer trail.

Figure 3-2:   Adjust your mouse to make it easier to use.

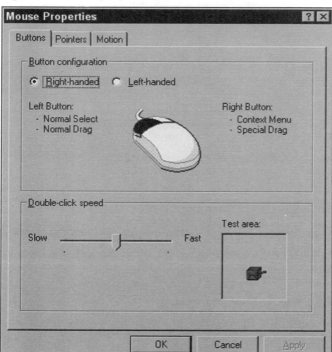

6. Click OK to close the dialog box and apply your changes.

Mastering Your Keyboard

As important as the mouse is in Windows 98, you also use your keyboard to interact with programs and to create documents.

Pressing special keys

You can use a lot of keyboard shortcuts in Windows 98. Table 3-1 shows many of the more popular shortcuts that can save you a lot of time. In the table, a plus sign (+) means that you hold down the first key as you press the second key.

**Table 3-1   Important Windows 98
           Keyboard Shortcuts**

Action	*Shortcut*
Activate a command on a menu	Alt+underlined letter
Activate a selected object	Enter
Cancel a menu or dialog box	Esc
Close the current program	Alt+F4
Close the current window	Ctrl+F4
Copy the selected object	Ctrl+C
Cut the selected object	Ctrl+X
Delete the selected object	Delete
Delete a file without placing it in the Recycle Bin	Shift+Delete
Display the Start menu	Ctrl+Esc (or Windows key)
Highlight the previous option on the list	Shift+Tab
Highlight the following option on the list	Tab
Open a Help window	F1
Paste an object you cut or copied	Ctrl+V
Prevent a CD from playing automatically	Shift while inserting the CD
Refresh the view	F5
Rename an item	F2
Select all items	Ctrl+A
Switch to the program you last used	Alt+Tab
Undo an action	Ctrl+Z

Simplifying your keyboard

Your PC keyboard can be adjusted to make typing easier:

1. Choose Start⇨Settings⇨Control Panel.

2. Click the Keyboard icon to open the Keyboard Properties dialog box (see Figure 3-3).

Figure 3-3: Adjust your keyboard to make it easier to use.

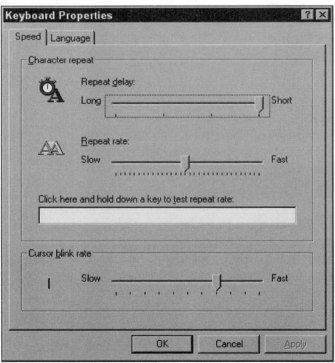

3. To set the amount of time a key must be held down before it begins repeating, drag the Repeat delay slider left for a long delay or right for a shorter delay.

4. Drag the Repeat rate slider left or right to adjust how quickly the same character repeats when a key is held down.

5. Drag the Cursor blink rate slider to adjust the frequency of the flashing of the cursor.

6. Click OK to confirm your changes and close the dialog box.

CHAPTER 4

ORGANIZING YOUR FILES

IN THIS CHAPTER

- Using Windows Explorer
- Using disks
- Finding files

One of the most frustrating things that you can encounter is doing hours of work, clicking the Save button, and then later not being able to figure out where your document went. And because modern PCs can store literally thousands of files in hundreds of different locations, hunting for your lost files can be as bad as looking for that needle in a haystack. In this chapter, you learn how to cut the task down to size so that you never have to worry about lost files again.

You also learn how to create and use folders and disks, which enable you to organize things the way you want and make it even easier for you to keep track of your work.

Using Windows Explorer

Windows Explorer is a program that you use to view the contents of all your disk drives as well as any resources on your network. You can do many things in Windows Explorer, including viewing, opening, copying, moving, deleting, and renaming files.

Looking at Windows Explorer

Windows Explorer normally displays two separate *panes* — windows within the Windows Explorer window. The left pane shows the *Folders Explorer Bar*. This is a structured view that shows the relationships between the disk drives and folders on your computer. The right pane — the contents pane — shows the items inside the currently selected folder. As you move around and select different folders, the contents pane changes to reflect the current folder.

Naming folders

Folders are where you store things on your disk drives. Folders can contain files, of course, but they can also contain additional folders. For example, the following *pathname* describes the location of a folder that is five levels deep in the folder structure:

```
C:\Windows\Start Menu\
Programs\Accessories\Entertainment
```

Each separate folder name is delineated by a backslash (\). In this case the drive is C:, and the folders are Windows, Start Menu, Programs, Accessories, and Entertainment. Each later folder is inside the preceding folder. That is, the Entertainment folder is inside the Accessories folder, and so on.

In Windows 98, you can name a file with up to 255 characters, including spaces. Filenames can't contain the following characters: \ / : * ? " < > | , and each filename must be unique within its folder. You can have two files with the same basic name only if they are in separate folders. Windows 98 warns you if you try to assign identical names to two files in the same folder.

Managing files

To open Windows Explorer, click the Start button and then select Programs⇨Windows Explorer. This opens the Windows Explorer window with disk drive C: selected. To select a different drive or folder, click the drive or folder in the Folders Explorer Bar. Folders have a horizontal line to their left that connects to the vertical line that extends down from above. The vertical line extends down from a drive or folder icon to connect to all the folders contained within the drive or folder. Some folders have a small box where the horizontal line to the left of the folder connects to the vertical line that tells you that the folder with the box contains additional folders. If the box contains a plus sign (+), those additional folders are not currently being displayed — the folder display is *collapsed*. A minus sign (-) indicates that the folder has been *expanded* to show the additional folders it contains. You can click the box to expand or collapse the display.

To select a folder to show in the contents pane, click the folder's icon. An open folder icon indicates the currently selected folder, while all other folders have a closed folder icon. Figure 4-1 shows how the Folders Explorer Bar appears when some folders are expanded, some are collapsed, and one folder is open.

Figure 4-1: Click in the Folders Explorer Bar to navigate the list of folders.

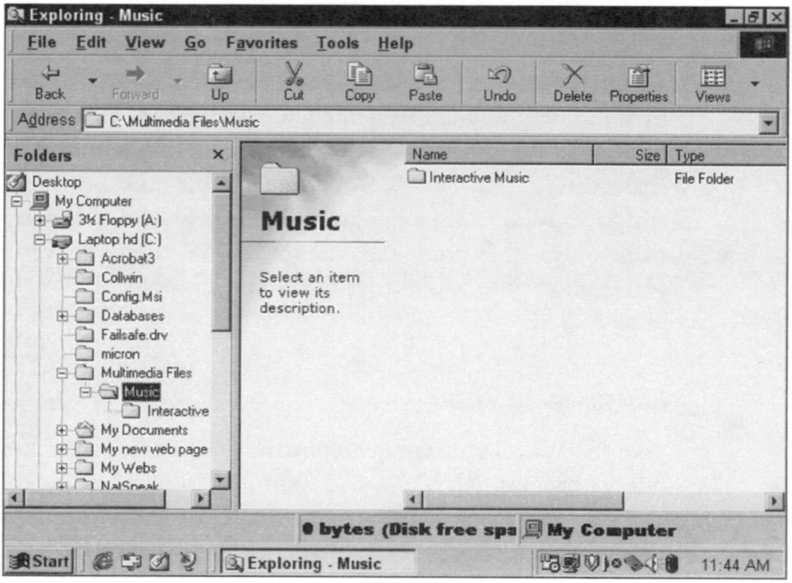

After you open a folder using the Folders Explorer Bar, you can switch over to the contents pane to work with individual files. To open a file, you can simply double-click the file (single-click if you have configured your system for single clicks). Here are some additional things you can do:

■ Select a file and press the F2 key if you want to rename the file. Be careful if the filename shows an *extension* — one to three characters following a period at the end of the name. Changing the extension can cause problems because Windows 98 uses the extension to determine how to open files.

■ Right-click a file to display a context-sensitive menu showing actions that you can perform on the file (see Figure 4-2). This menu varies depending on the type of file you select.

Figure 4-2:   Right-click to choose appropriate options.

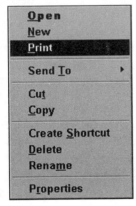

■ Right-click a file and select Send To⇨3½ Floppy (A), to save a copy of the file on a removable disk in drive A:. Don't try this with very large files because removable disks have limited space.

■ Use the drag-and-drop techniques you learned in Chapter 3 to copy or move files to new locations.

- Select a file and press the Delete key to send the file to the Windows 98 Recycle Bin. In Chapter 5, you learn how to work with the Recycle Bin so that you can recover files you accidentally deleted.

Be especially careful in deleting, moving, or renaming files. Unless the file is one that you created, you can cause severe problems by doing any of these things to unknown files. In extreme cases, you may cause some programs to fail or possibly even prevent Windows 98 itself from running.

Viewing folders

The contents pane can display the file and folder icons several different ways. You can change the display so that it shows the largest number of icons in the smallest space, or you may want to see as many details about each file as possible.

To change the view type, select View and then choose one of the following options:

- *Large Icons* to display each file or folder in alphabetically arranged horizontal rows using the same size icons that appear on the Windows 98 desktop. All folder icons appear before any file icons.

- *Small Icons* to display the icons in a similar manner, but using much smaller icons that require far less space. Note, however, that in Small Icon view the entire filename is shown rather than the abbreviated filename shown in Large Icon view, so you may not see any more icons than in Large Icon view.

- *List* to display the icons in a similar manner as the Small Icon view, except that the icons are arranged in vertical columns rather than horizontal rows.

■ *Details* to display the icons in a vertical column along with additional columns that provide details, such as the size, type, and date of the files. In Details view, you can choose the display sort order by clicking one of the column headings. You can reverse the order by clicking the same column heading a second time.

Customizing the display

You have several other options for change the way Windows Explorer displays files and folders, as shown in Figure 4-3. Some of these settings are far more useful than others. Here are some that you may want to know about:

Figure 4-3:   Use the View menu to customize the display.

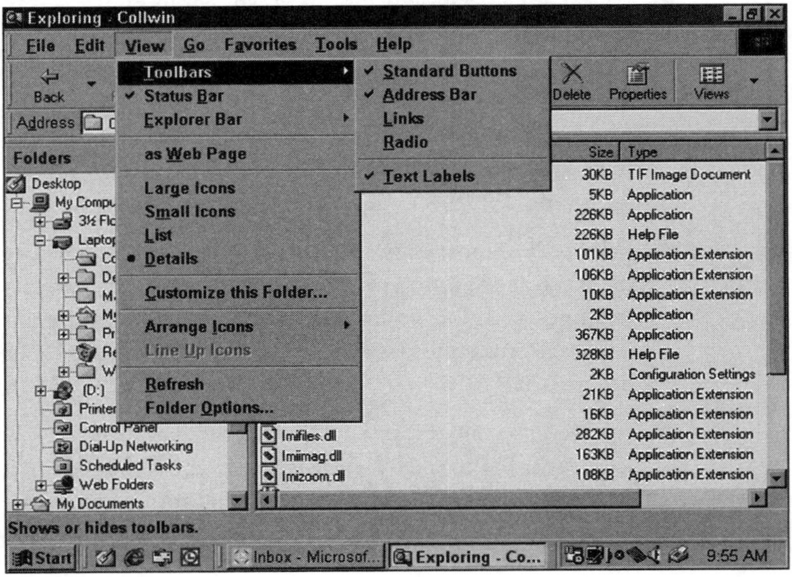

■ Select View➪Toolbars➪Text Labels to toggle the display of the button labels on the toolbar. Removing the labels shrinks the toolbar. You can always view the name of a toolbar button by holding the mouse pointer over the button for a short time.

■ Select View➪Toolbars➪Address Bar to toggle the display of the Address Bar.

■ Select View➪as Web Page to view thumbnail previews of selected files. This works best when you're viewing a folder that contains graphics files because you don't have to open the individual files in order to see their contents.

■ Select View➪Arrange Icons to select a different sort order for the current folder.

■ Select View➪Folder Options, as shown in Figure 4-4 to display the Folder Options dialog box. Click the View tab to select from the advanced options for viewing the files. To learn about any of the advanced settings, click the question mark in the Folder Options dialog box title bar, and then click an option with the question mark pointer.

■ Move the mouse pointer over the vertical divider between the Windows Explorer panes. When the pointer changes to a double-headed arrow, hold down the left mouse button and drag the divider left or right to resize the panes.

■ In Details view, drag the column dividers to resize the columns. Double-click the divider at the right edge of a column to automatically resize the column to show the longest entry.

■ To create the maximum space for the contents pane, click the Close button at the top of the Folders Explorer Bar. You can use View➪Explorer Bar➪Folders to redisplay the Folders Explorer Bar when necessary.

Figure 4-4:   Use the View tab to control what is displayed.

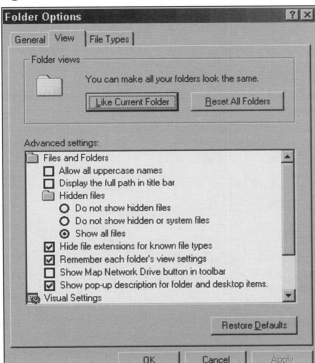

Adding folders

If you use a filing cabinet to organize your paperwork, you probably use different folders to keep each project separate from the others. The same idea applies to the documents that you store on your computer. You can create new folders to help organize your files so you can more easily find what you need.

You can create new folders anywhere on your PC's disk drives, but you need to be aware of one limitation on creating new folders: The *root* folder — the unnamed folder at the lowest level of a disk drive (C:\, for example) — has a limited capacity. You're probably safe if you keep the number of root folder entries under about 100.

The best way to deal with the limitation on root folder entries is to use a different folder as the basis for your new folders. One good starting point is the My Documents folder where you can create as many new folders as necessary to organize your document files for different projects.

Creating a new folder in Windows 98 is very easy. Follow these steps:

1. Open Windows Explorer.

2. In the Folders Explorer Bar, select the folder that you want as the parent of the new folder. This is the folder that will contain your new folder.

3. Select File➪New➪Folder. This creates a folder named New Folder. The name of the new folder is highlighted in the Windows Explorer contents pane.

4. Type a new name for the folder and press Enter.

Arranging folders

You can move folders in Windows Explorer the same way that you move individual files. Dragging and dropping folders is generally the easiest way to move them, but you can also select a folder, click the Cut button, select the new parent folder, and click the Paste button.

Moving a folder also moves everything in the folder. If what you really want to do is move the folder's contents but not the folder itself, first select the folder in the Folders Explorer Bar. Next press Ctrl+A to select everything in the folder. Now you can use the drag-and-drop or cut-and-paste methods to move the selected items, leaving the folder in place.

You can safely move your document files, but if you move other types of files, you may create problems, such as preventing some programs from running properly. If you need to move a program file, uninstalling the program and then later reinstalling it in the new location is generally the safest way to go. For more info on adding new programs, see Chapter 8.

Using Disks

Almost every PC houses three different types of disk drives. Typically, drive A: is a 3½ inch removable disk known as a *floppy disk* or a *diskette*. Most PCs skip drive B:, although if this drive is present it is like drive A:. Drive C: is a *hard disk* and has a capacity several thousand times that of drive A:. Both of these types of drives are used to store program and document files and are typically available for saving files.

The third common type of drive is the CD-ROM drive, and this is often designated as drive D:. CD-ROMs look very much like audio CDs and are mostly used as a means of distributing software. In most PCs, the CD-ROM drive is a *read-only* drive — you can read information from the drive but can't save anything to it. Variations on the CD-ROM drive, including CD-R and CD-RW drives, can write to special discs that can be recorded on. Some newer PCs include DVD drives, which use a special high capacity disc.

In addition to these common types of disk drives, some PCs use other types of disk drives, such as Zip drives. Essentially, these other types of drives are simply much higher capacity replacements for floppy disks. You can only use these alternative disks if your system is equipped with the correct type of drive.

Preparing disks for use

You must *format* disks before you can use them. Formatting is the process of writing electronic markers on the disk so your system knows where to write the data.

Before you format a disk you should be aware of one very important fact — formatting erases everything that is currently on the disk. Don't format a disk unless you're certain that you won't need anything that is on the disk.

If you do want to format a disk, follow these steps:

1. Place the disk you want to format in drive A:.

2. Open Windows Explorer.

3. In the Folders Explorer Bar, right-click the icon for 3½ Floppy (A:). You may need to scroll up a bit to see this icon.

4. Select Format from the pop-up menu, as shown in Figure 4-5.

Figure 4-5:   Select Format to format the selected disk.

| **Explore** |
| **Open** |
| **Find...** |
| **Copy Disk...** |
| **Sharing...** |
| **Format...** |
| **Create Shortcut** |
| **Properties** |

5. Select the type of format you wish to use:

Quick (erase) simply removes any existing files by marking the space that they occupy as available. You can't use this option if the disk has never been formatted.

Full performs a complete format. This is the best option to choose if you will be storing critical files on the disk because this also checks for errors on the disk.

Copy system files only does not format the disk. Rather, it creates a disk that you can use to start your computer in an emergency.

6. Type a name of up to 11 characters in the label box. This disk label may help you identify the disk later.

7. Click the Start button to begin formatting the disk.

8. Wait until the format is complete before you click the Close button.

If the *Display summary when finished* check box is checked, Windows 98 shows you the results of the formatting process. As a general rule, discard any disks that show errors during a format.

Increasing disk performance

Because disk drives are mechanical components, they are often some of the slowest parts of your PC. Any improvements that you can make to their performance may have a much larger effect on the overall performance of your entire computer system.

In this section, we look at some of the tools that Windows 98 provides specifically to help out your disk drives. You can do even more by remembering to delete old files you no longer need and by resisting the urge to continually add new programs that you don't need to your system.

Here's how you access the Windows 98 disk tools:

1. Open Windows Explorer.

2. In the Folders Explorer Bar, right-click the drive icon for the drive you want to improve (typically drive C:).

3. Select Properties from the pop-up menu to display the Properties dialog box for the selected disk.

4. On the General tab, click the Disk Cleanup button.

5. Make certain that all the check boxes are checked and then click OK.

6. Click Yes to remove the extra files.

7. When you return to the Properties dialog box, click the Tools tab.

8. Click the Check Now button to start the ScanDisk tool. ScanDisk checks to make certain your disk doesn't have any errors that could cause you to lose data.

9. Make certain the Automatically fix errors check box is checked and then click the Start button in the ScanDisk dialog box.

10. Click the Close button when ScanDisk finishes checking your disk.

11. Click the Defragment Now button to start the disk defragmenter tool. This improves your disk performance by making each file's data *contiguous* (located together) on the hard disk. Defragmenting your hard disk goes much faster if no other programs are running at the same time.

12. Click the Close button when the defragmentation is complete.

13. Click the OK button to close the Properties dialog box.

You can also have Windows 98 automatically run the tools to improve your disk performance. Click the Windows 98 Start button and then choose Accessories➪System Tools➪Maintenance Wizard. Go through the steps suggested by the wizard to set up a schedule for running these tasks on a regular basis. Be sure to choose a time when you won't be using your PC, but when your computer will be powered on.

Finding Files

With the Windows 98 Find tool you can find almost anything on your computer. Here are some examples of the types of searches you can perform using the Find tool:

■ You can search for a file even if you only know part of the filename.

■ You can find files that were modified within a specific time period.

■ You can locate all files of a specific type.

■ You can look for files that contain specific text.

■ You can search for files of a certain size.

Here's how to use the Find tool on your system:

1. Choose Start➪Find➪Files or Folders to display the Find dialog box.

2. Enter the search criteria you need in the various text boxes on the three tabs of the dialog box.

Remember that the located files must meet each condition you specify. Start out simple and then restrict the search by adding more conditions if your search produces too many results.

3. Click the Find Now button to begin the search. Depending on the number of files on the drives being searched, the search may take several minutes.

4. If you need to further restrict your search while retaining all the current search conditions, add those new conditions to the appropriate text boxes and click Find Now again without clicking the New Search button. Clicking New Search clears the search conditions.

5. If you begin a new search by clicking the New Search button, be sure to check the location that is shown in the Look in list box.

After you locate the file you want, you can work with the file directly in the Find dialog box. If you want to open a file, double-click its name in the file list. You can also right-click the files in the list to display the pop-up context menu so that you can rename, delete, cut, or copy them. Depending on the file type, you may have additional options available.

CHAPTER 5

SAVING AND OPENING YOUR WORK

IN THIS CHAPTER

- Saving your files
- Starting your documents

No matter how much you paid for your PC, its value is probably a tiny fraction of the value of the work that you do on the system. Your documents represent many hours of work — possibly thousands of hours — and would be far harder to replace than your entire computer system. In this chapter, you learn how to make certain that your documents are safe and accessible.

Saving Your Files

When you begin creating a document on your PC, the document exists only in the computer's random access memory (RAM). If you don't save your work onto one of your disk drives, the document completely disappears as soon as you power down the computer.

New computer users often experience a certain amount of confusion regarding the difference between *offline* storage — such as disk drives — and memory. Offline storage holds data that won't disappear when the computer is turned off. Memory is the computer's workspace — the place where programs and data must be moved so the computer can work with them.

Remember

Memory and disk space serve quite different purposes. If you don't remember anything else about the two, at least remember that your documents aren't safe until you've saved them to disk.

Saving to the My Documents folder

Windows 98 automatically creates a folder that is intended as the storage location for your document files. The pathname of this folder is C:\My Documents.

The My Documents folder is intended as the storage location for all types of document files. Windows 98 usually recognizes which application created each type of document, so there's not much confusion when storing different types of files in this folder, either.

Most programs that were designed for Windows 98 automatically offer the My Documents folder as the default location for saving your files.

If the My Documents folder does not automatically appear as the destination when you save files, you can probably change the default location so that all your documents are saved in the same location. Each program that you use may use slightly different commands for setting the default file locations. In Microsoft Word, for example, you select Tools⇨Options and then click the File Locations tab.

Just because you use the My Documents folder as the default file location doesn't mean that you have to keep everything in one folder. Creating project folders within the My Documents folder is often better, as discussed in Chapter 4.

How often should you save your files? The answer to that is pretty simple — how much work do you want to redo if a problem occurs? If you're comfortable with losing a whole day of work, then save your work once a day. Personally, I click the Save button every ten to fifteen minutes.

Warning

Some programs can automatically save your work. If you decide to depend on this feature, make sure you know how to activate the feature — and how to recover the saved copy.

Saving another copy

An existing document is often a great starting point for a new document. This is especially true if your new document will be using the same structure or some of the same content as an existing document.

That's one of the ideas behind saving a document under a new name. You simply save the document under a different name, delete the information that isn't appropriate to the new document, and save yourself a bunch of work. Use the File⇨Save As command and then specify a new filename to create a copy of an existing document.

Creating a new document from an old document isn't the only reason to save a document as a different document. You may also want to use information in a different program. But because different application programs use different *file formats*, you may need to use the File⇨Save As command to change the document to a different type of document. If you don't find the other program's native format, you can always choose to save the file as plain text. You lose any fancy formatting, but your data will be intact. Virtually all Windows 98 programs can read and write plain-text files.

Copying files to removable disks

Modern PCs are pretty foolproof, but that doesn't mean that accidents can't happen. Because disk drives are mechanical components, they can fail and take all your carefully saved document files with them.

One of the best ways to protect yourself from either mechanical failure or from brain fade is to have a backup copy of your important document files. Disasters almost always seem to affect the only copy you have of a file.

You can save document files onto floppy disks in several ways. Unfortunately, the easiest of these ways may not be the best.

The most straightforward method of saving document files onto a floppy disk is to select drive A: as the destination after you select File⇨Save As. When you do so, most programs tend to set the default file location to drive A:. As a result, any new files that you save are also saved onto the floppy disk, and if you attempt to open an existing file, the program insists on looking for that file on drive A: as well. You may even discover that the program remembers where you last saved a file when you later reopen the program, so it again insists on looking to drive A:.

A better way to save document files onto a floppy disk is to save the file as usual in the My Documents folder. When you close the document, use Windows Explorer to open the My Documents folder. Right-click the document file that you want to copy to a floppy disk and choose Send To⇨ 3½ Floppy (A). Because this method doesn't change any of the application's default settings, you don't have to hassle with changing anything back to what you really want.

Moving the My Documents folder

If you prefer that your default documents folder be located someplace other than in the My Documents folder, you can change the location to suit your needs.

Because the My Documents folder is used as the default document folder by most Windows 98 programs, you want to specify the new folder location correctly so that your programs use the correct folder. Here's the correct method for changing the location of the My Documents folder:

1. Right-click the My Documents icon on your desktop.

2. Choose Properties from the pop-up context menu, as shown in Figure 5-1.

Figure 5-1:   Use the My Documents Properties dialog box to correctly move the My Documents folder.

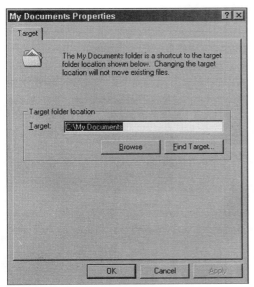

3. Enter the new location in the Target text box.

   If necessary, use the Browse or Find Target buttons to locate the correct folder.

4. Click OK to confirm your change.

5. Open Windows Explorer and move the files from your old My Documents folder to the new folder.

   This step is necessary because specifying a new location in Step 3 does not move your existing files.

Be sure to verify the location the next time you save files to make certain that the programs use the correct folder.

Starting Your Documents

You can open documents several ways in Windows 98. The following sections show you how to use the most popular methods.

Starting recent files

Windows 98 keeps a convenient list of your most recently used documents so that these files are the easiest to open.

To see the list of your recent documents, click the Start button and then highlight Documents on the Start menu; the list of documents appears. When you select an item from the list, Windows 98 opens the appropriate application and your document.

Emptying the Recent Documents list

As convenient as the recent documents list may be, it's also a record that's available for anyone who wants to snoop and see just what you've been working on.

If you think you're safe from people looking at your recent documents list simply because no one else uses your PC, you may be surprised to learn that this list may also be available to others if your computer is on a network. Someone could simply browse your C:\Windows\Recent folder from anywhere on the network and instantly see which documents you've been using — and you would never know that they had been looking over your shoulder!

Items on the recent documents list are *shortcuts* to the actual documents. Deleting the shortcut has no effect on the document itself. Conversely, deleting or moving the document file has no effect on the existing shortcut. If you accidentally delete a document file, the shortcut remains on the recent documents list — which may make you think that your document is still safe.

You can clear individual items from the recent documents list or you can go all the way and take everything off the list. To clear items one at a time, follow these steps:

1. Click the Start button.

2. Highlight Documents to open the most recently used documents list.

3. Right-click the item that you wish to remove and choose Delete. Hold down the Shift key if you don't want the shortcut moved to the Recycle Bin.

To quickly clear the entire list, follow these steps:

1. Right-click the Windows 98 taskbar.

2. Choose Properties to display the Taskbar Properties dialog box.

3. Click the Start Menu Programs tab to bring the tab to the front.

4. Click the Clear button to remove your entire list of document shortcuts. This step doesn't send the shortcuts to the Recycle Bin, so be certain that you want to completely clear the list before you click the button.

5. Click the OK button to close the dialog box.

Clearing out the recent documents list may not remove all traces of the files that you've been using. Most Windows 98 programs also keep a list of recent documents at the bottom of their File menu. In addition, programs such as Microsoft Outlook may keep an additional record of the document files you've used.

Starting from the My Documents folder

Because the recently used documents list is limited to about 15 entries, you probably have a lot of documents that aren't on the list. You can still easily open any of those document files by first opening the My Documents folder.

You can open the My Documents folder several different ways:

■ You can use the My Documents icon if it appears on your desktop.

■ You can use Windows Explorer to open the C:\My Documents folder.

■ You can also open the folder by selecting My Documents from the top of the recently used documents list on the Start menu.

After you open the My Documents folder, you can simply double-click (or single-click depending on how your system is configured) the document file you wish to open. Because Windows 98 remembers the correct program to use, you don't have to worry about the document type.

Starting files by clicking

If you already have an application program open, you can open the program's documents directly from within the program. In most programs, you may discover the following options:

■ Nearly all programs have a File⇨Open command that displays a File Open dialog box. Use this dialog box to select the files that you wish to open and then click the Open button.

■ Many programs include an Open icon on their Standard toolbar, which also displays the File Open dialog box.

■ You may also see a list of recently used files at the bottom of a program's File menu. Click the file you want to open it without going through the File Open dialog box.

Starting files by dragging

Although Windows 98 tries to remember the correct program to use for opening most document files, sometimes it tries to open a file using the wrong program. You may have changed the file extension. Also, you may have installed a new program that Windows 98 associated with one of your existing file extensions. Or perhaps you just want to use a different program to open a file in a special case.

In Windows 98, you can open files using one of the following techniques:

■ Point to the file that you wish to open, hold down the left mouse button, drag the file onto the program you wish to use to open the file, and release the mouse button to drop the file.

■ If the target program is open, you drop the file onto the program's window.

■ If you can't see the window, move the mouse pointer onto the program's taskbar button, wait for the program window to open, and then drop the file on the window.

■ If the target program is not open, you can drop the document file onto the program's icon.

Recycling Files

The Recycle Bin is a special folder that Windows 98 creates on each hard disk. When you delete files from within the Windows 98 graphical user interface, those deleted files are actually moved to the Recycle Bin instead of being physically deleted. This provides you with a second chance in case you delete a file in error.

Although deleted files are normally moved to the Recycle Bin, in the following cases, files are actually deleted immediately and you can't restore them from the Recycle Bin:

■ Files that you delete from the MS-DOS Prompt command line are not sent to the Recycle Bin.

■ Files that you delete while holding down the Shift key are not sent to the Recycle Bin.

■ If the *Do not move files to the Recycle Bin* check box in the Recycle Bin Properties dialog box is selected, no files are sent to the Recycle Bin. See "Controlling the Recycle Bin" later in this chapter for details.

Recovering files from the Recycle Bin

If you have accidentally deleted a file, the first place you want to go is to the Recycle Bin to restore the file to its original location. Don't delay too long because the oldest files in the Recycle Bin can be automatically deleted if the Recycle Bin becomes too crowded.

To restore files that you have accidentally deleted, follow these steps:

1. Open the Recycle Bin by double-clicking (or single-clicking as appropriate) the Recycle Bin icon on your desktop.

2. Right-click the item that you wish to restore.

3. Select Restore from the pop-up context menu as shown in Figure 5-2.

4. Click the Close button to close the Recycle Bin.

Restored files are always restored to their original location, which can be a problem if you already created a new file with the same name in that location. If this is the case, rename the new file before you restore the deleted one.

Figure 5-2:   The Recycle Bin gives you a second chance when you accidentally delete files.

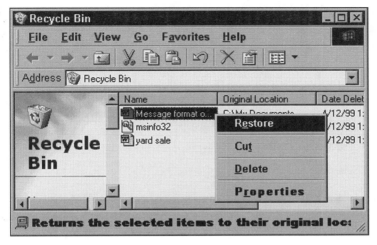

Emptying the Recycle Bin

The files that are in the Recycle Bin use disk space. But even if you have plenty of room, there are good reasons for emptying the Recycle Bin. If the Recycle Bin gets too full, you may not be able to recover important files because they aren't in the Recycle Bin anymore. Another reason is simply that you probably really do want some files to go away.

You have two ways to empty the Recycle Bin:

- If you want to completely remove all files from the Recycle Bin, select File⇨Empty Recycle Bin or click the Empty Recycle Bin link that appears when you first open the Recycle Bin. You can also right-click the Recycle Bin icon on your desktop and choose Empty Recycle Bin from the pop-up context menu.

- If you want to selectively remove files from the Recycle Bin, open the Recycle Bin and select the files that you want to remove. Then right-click the selected files and choose Delete from the pop-up context menu.

CHAPTER 6

PERSONALIZING YOUR SCREEN

IN THIS CHAPTER

- Personalizing your screen
- Arranging your desktop
- Personalizing your Start menu
- Starting screen savers

Windows 98 really puts the "personal" into personal computers. Almost every part of the Windows 98 appearance is customizable.

Wanting a unique desktop is only one reason why you may want to change the look of Windows 98. You may also want to make changes to improve the readability of your screen. You may need to improve the contrast on a low-quality laptop display. Or perhaps you would like to have all the PCs in a public area of your office present a very dignified corporate image.

Regardless your reasons for wanting to change the appearance of Windows 98, you learn how to make those changes in this chapter.

Personalizing Your Screen

Microsoft has concentrated most of the visual settings options for Windows 98 into one dialog box — the Display Properties dialog box. Right-click a blank area of your desktop and choose Properties from the pop-up context menu to display this dialog box.

The following sections cover the most common screen settings options (except for the screen saver options, which are covered later in this chapter). Your Display Properties dialog box may include options not covered here.

Selecting the background image

You use the Background tab, as shown in Figure 6-1, to choose a background image to appear on your desktop.

Figure 6-1: Use the Display Properties dialog box to change the Windows 98 appearance settings.

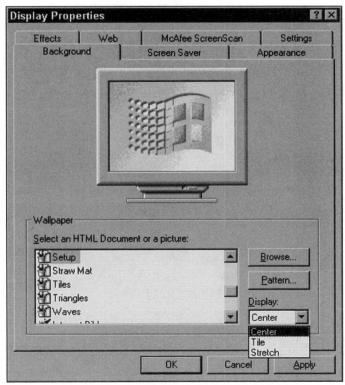

You can choose an image file to use as a background (or *wallpaper*) by selecting it from the list box or by clicking the Browse button and selecting a file on your hard disk. Windows 98 can use files that are in *Windows bitmap* format — files with a BMP extension — directly. If you choose an HTML document (HTM extension) or a JPEG image (JPG extension), you must allow Windows 98 to activate the *Active Desktop* feature. If you choose an image file that does not completely fill the desktop, you can select an option from the drop-down Display list box. Centering the image places it in the middle of the screen with your standard background color around the edges. Tiling the image places multiple copies of the image on the desktop. Stretching the image expands the image to fill the entire desktop. If you change the screen resolution, you may need to readjust the image settings to get the look you prefer.

If you would rather use a pattern instead of an image file for the background, click the Pattern button and choose the pattern you prefer. If you choose a background image and a pattern, the pattern only appears outside the edges of the background image.

Any background image or pattern that you select appears behind everything else on your desktop. That is, the image or pattern won't hide the desktop icons.

Click Apply to apply any changes you've made before moving from one tab to another. Keeping track of your changes is far easier if you make a few at a time.

Changing lettering

On the Appearance tab of the Display Properties dialog box, shown in Figure 6-2, you can change the colors and font settings that Windows 98 uses.

Figure 6-2:   Use the Display Properties dialog box to control options that affect how your screen looks.

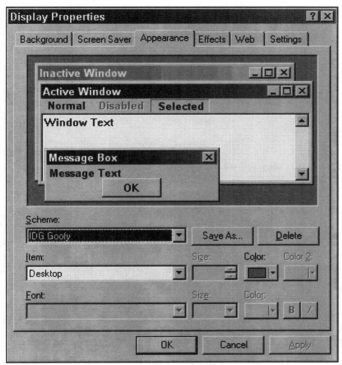

Before you make any changes on this tab, click the Save As button and save your current settings. This enables you to return to your original settings at any time with just a few mouse clicks.

Click the down arrow at the right edge of the Scheme list box to try out one of the predefined color and font settings. If you save your own settings, you find those settings listed in this list box as well.

You can click an item in the sample area to change the item's settings, or you can select items by name in the Item list box.

A few items can only be adjusted by selecting them from the list box. Depending on the item that you have selected, you may have several options that you can adjust. These include color settings and font settings for some items.

After you create a new set of color and font selections, be sure to use the Save As button to save those settings. After you create several sets of named settings, switching between them and choosing the one that you really like becomes much easier.

Adding special effects

On the Effects tab, shown in Figure 6-3, you find a number of interesting options:

Figure 6-3: Use the Effects tab to add special effects.

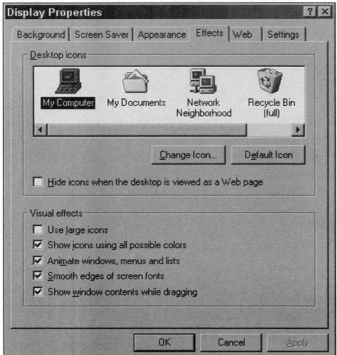

- Select one of the standard desktop icons from the list box and then click the Change Icon button if you would like to choose your own desktop icons. Click the Default Icon button to return an icon to its original appearance.

- Check the *Hide icons when the desktop is viewed as a web page* check box if you have an HTML document that you use as your desktop and do not want icons to appear on top of that document.

- Select the *Use large icons* check box if you want Windows 98 to use icons that are about twice the normal size on your desktop.

- Select the *Show icons using all possible colors* check box to make the icons as colorful as possible.

- Select the *Animate windows, menus and lists* check box to make those screen elements slide into place rather than simply appearing.

- Select the *Smooth edges of screen fonts* check box to improve the appearance of text — especially in the larger sizes — that appears on your screen.

- Select the *Show window contents while dragging* check box to show on-screen windows while they're being moved around the screen. If this option is not selected, you only see an outline of the window as you drag the window.

Sharpening the picture

On the Settings tab, you can adjust the number of colors that are displayed and the screen resolution.

The range of options on this tab depend on the display adapter installed in your system and on the monitor that you use. The two settings on this tab are interrelated. That is, if you choose a very high setting on one option, you may not be able to choose the setting you want on the other.

The Colors drop-down list box enables you to choose the number of colors that can be displayed at one time. Photographic images generally appear more lifelike when more colors are displayed.

The Screen area slider enables you to choose the screen resolution, as shown in Figure 6-4. Higher resolution settings enable you to have more things on the screen at the same time.

Figure 6-4: Use the Settings tab to adjust color levels and resolution.

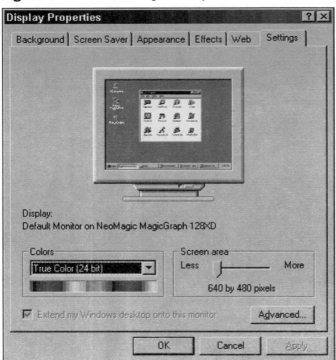

When you click the Apply button to change your screen resolution and number of colors, Windows 98 resizes the screen and asks if you want to keep the new settings. If you do not confirm that you want to keep the new settings within 15 seconds, Windows 98 restores your old settings. In a few cases, you may need to restart your computer to apply the new settings.

Improving picture performance

Clicking on the Advanced button near the bottom of the Settings tab displays a Properties dialog box that enables you to change your display adapter and monitor and to make some additional settings that can improve how your video components perform. The Properties dialog box varies according to the display adapter installed in your system, but here are some of the more common settings that you may see:

■ On the General tab, make certain that the *Show settings icon on task bar* check box is selected. This setting displays a small icon in the System Tray that you can then click to choose between the available screen color depth and resolution settings.

■ On the Adapter tab, the Change button enables you to select a different display adapter. If your color depth setting is stuck at 16 colors and your resolution setting is stuck at 640x480 or 800x600, you may have your adapter specified incorrectly. You should choose the correct brand and model of display adapter rather than VGA or SVGA.

■ If the Adapter tab includes a Refresh rate setting, you may be able to reduce flicker by choosing a higher refresh rate. You must choose a setting that is compatible with your monitor to prevent damage to your monitor, but you should choose a setting of at least 72Hz if possible.

■ On the Monitor tab, the Change button enables you to specify the correct brand and model of your monitor.

■ The Performance tab includes a slider that you can use to adjust the level of hardware-assisted graphics acceleration that is used.

■ The Color Management tab enables you to select a color profile that ensures that the on-screen colors are as true to life as possible.

Making your desktop look like a Web page

On the Web tab of the Display Properties dialog box, you can choose to view your desktop as a Web page, which enables you to use both HTML documents and JPEG image files as the background for your desktop.

You can also choose to add active content to your desktop by selecting an item from the list box or by clicking the New button and visiting the related Microsoft Web site. When you have finished making all your display setting changes, click OK to close the Display Properties dialog box.

Arranging Your Desktop

You can bring some order to your Windows 98 desktop by using a few simple options:

■ You can drag and drop icons on your desktop to rearrange them.

■ You can right-click a blank space on the desktop and choose Line Up Icons from the pop-up context menu to move the icons into orderly columns with the icons evenly spaced.

■ You can right-click a blank space on the desktop and choose Arrange Icons and then choose a sort order to sort the icons by name, type, size, or date.

■ You can right-click a blank space on the desktop and choose Arrange Icons⇨Auto Arrange to automatically line up the icons whenever a new icon is added, an existing icon is deleted, or icons are dropped into the middle of existing icons.

You can adjust the icon spacing by following these steps:

1. Open the Display Properties dialog box by right-clicking a blank space on the desktop and choosing Properties.

2. Click the Appearance tab.

3. In the Item list box, select Icon Spacing (Horizontal) to specify the width between columns of icons or Icon Spacing (Vertical) to specify the vertical spacing between icon rows.

4. Use the Size spin control to adjust the spacing up or down as desired.

5. Click OK to close the dialog box and confirm your changes.

If you choose to use the Auto Arrange option, you can rearrange the order of the icons by dragging icons and dropping them between two existing icons. The lower of the existing icons (and all remaining icons) move down (or to the top of the next column) to make room for the new icon.

Personalizing Your Start Menu

Your Start menu is probably the primary way that you access your programs. If your menu starts looking like the one in Figure 6-5, with too many items to display on one screen, finding and opening the items that you want to use may become difficult.

Figure 6-5: If your menu becomes too crowded, it's time to organize things.

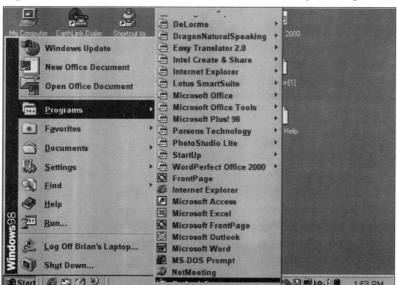

Okay, technically speaking most of the rearrangement that you can do is on the Programs menu rather than on the base Start menu. Still, you can move any items that appear above Programs on the Start menu.

As soon as you make manual changes to the menus, Windows 98 stops doing automatic menu organization. By default, Windows 98 displays items on the menus in alphabetical order, with submenus at the top of each menu. After you make a manual change to the menus, Windows 98 allows items to appear in any order on the menus.

Dragging and dropping

One method of rearranging your menu is to drag and drop items. You can only move items to existing menus using drag and drop — you can't create additional menus using this method.

To move an item to a new menu location using drag and drop, point to the item that you wish to move, hold down the left mouse button, and drag it to the new location. Release the mouse button to drop the item. If you want to move something to a different menu level, drag the item onto the menu and wait for the menu to open. Move the mouse pointer to the desired destination and drop the item.

You can also drag and drop things onto the Start menu from your desktop or from Windows Explorer.

Exploring your Start menu

Although the drag and drop method is a convenient way to quickly rearrange a few items on your Start menu, it's not as easy to use when you want to move a number of items. For this, a far better method is to explore your Start menu.

To explore your Start menu, begin by right-clicking the Start button. Choose Explore from the pop-up context menu, which opens Windows Explorer with the C:\Windows\Start Menu folder open. This folder contains any items that appear above Programs on the Start menu as well as the Programs folder itself. Click the plus sign in the box to the left of the Programs folder to expand the display, and then click the Programs folder in the Folders Explorer Bar to display the contents of the Programs folder.

After you open the Programs folder, you can move items, create new folders, and generally rearrange the folder items as you see fit. Any changes you make are reflected in the menus when you next open the Start menu.

Although the Programs folder is very much like any other folder on your PC, you should be aware of some special characteristics:

■ You should only place *shortcuts* and folders within the Programs folder and its subfolders. Never place actual programs in the Programs folder or on your desktop.

■ Any items that are placed in the StartUp folder in the Programs folder automatically run when you start Windows 98.

■ Windows Explorer won't necessarily show you the order in which items appear on the menu. Because Windows 98 stops maintaining the menu order as soon as you begin moving things around on your own, you may need to use a combination of exploring your Start menu to make big changes, and then later using drag and drop on the menu to fine-tune the display order.

For more information on using Windows Explorer, see Chapter 4.

Starting Screen Savers

Modern PCs simply don't need *screen savers*. Unlike some PCs many years ago, modern monitors do not suffer damage by having an unchanging image displayed on the screen.

Screen savers can serve one semi-useful purpose. If you specify a password, someone needs the correct password to disable the screen saver and view your desktop unless they turn your system off and back on.

Installing a screen saver

Windows 98 includes a number of screen savers that you can choose. You may want to check to verify that all the optional screen savers are installed. To do so, follow these steps:

1. Choose Start⇨Settings⇨Control Panel.

2. Open the Add/Remove Programs item.

3. Click the Windows Setup tab to bring the tab to the front.

4. Select Accessories and click the Details button.

5. Scroll down to select Screen Savers and click the Details button.

6. If all three sets of screen savers are not checked, you may wish to select them now so they will be installed.

7. Click OK in each dialog box to close the dialog boxes.

You may need to insert your Windows 98 CD-ROM so that the additional screen savers can be installed.

Choosing a screen saver

After you install the screen savers on your system, you can choose one to use. To select a screen saver, right-click a blank space on your desktop and choose Properties from the pop-up context menu. Click the Screen Saver tab to bring it to the front, as shown in Figure 6-6.

Next, click the down arrow at the right side of the Screen Saver list box and choose an option from the list. To see a full-screen preview of the screen saver, click the Preview button.

Be careful not to move your mouse or press any keys until you finish viewing the full-screen preview.

Figure 6-6: Choose a screen saver to make your screen a little more interesting.

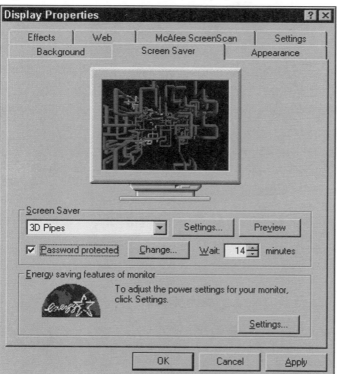

Customizing a screen saver

You can adjust many screen savers to make them a little more personal. Often, you can change the speed, the texture, the size, and the motion of the objects that are drawn on the screen. Screen savers that display text can generally use custom text that you specify. The settings vary according to which screen saver you select, but in each case, clicking the Settings button displays a setup dialog box for the screen saver.

In addition to the settings that vary according to the selected screen saver, one setting applies no matter which screen saver you choose: the Wait setting, which specifies how long Windows 98 waits after you stop using your PC before it displays the screen saver. The waiting time restarts whenever you press a key or move your mouse, so if you ever want to see the screen saver, you may want to specify a short waiting time. Use the up or down arrows at the right edge of the Wait spin box to select the waiting time.

Setting your password

If you use a screen saver, you can specify a password that someone must enter in order to close the screen saver. When a password is in effect, pressing a key or moving the mouse displays a dialog box asking for the password. If the correct password is not entered in the dialog box, the Windows 98 desktop is not restored.

Unfortunately, screen saver passwords offer little real protection because someone could simply shut down and restart the computer to bypass this minimal level of security.

If you do want to use a password to at least keep casual snoops away from your system, follow these steps:

1. Add a check to the Password protected check box.

2. Click the Change button to display the Change Password dialog box.

3. Enter the same password in both text boxes. The password that you type doesn't appear — asterisks are shown in place of each character.

4. Click OK to close the dialog box.

Be sure to remember your password exactly. If you forget your password, you can't close the screen saver without shutting down your system, and you won't be able to specify a new password.

CHAPTER 7

CONNECTING TO THE INTERNET

IN THIS CHAPTER

- Understanding the Internet
- Understanding what you need
- Setting up your account
- Going online
- Visiting Web sites
- Finding things online

It's probably a safe bet that most people would mention getting on the Internet as one of the most exciting reasons for getting a PC. In this chapter, you learn the basics of what the Internet is, what you need for getting onto the Internet, and a little about using the Internet. You won't learn all there is to know about the Internet in such a brief discussion, but at least you can get started.

Understanding the Internet

The Internet is really just a huge *network* that connects millions of computers all around the world. Traditional computer networks generally include a fairly stable and limited number of computers — often within a single organization, such as a company or a university. The Internet really turns this traditional view upside down. On the Internet, computers connect and disconnect, and no one organization owns the Internet.

An Internet history lesson

Originally, the network that has become the Internet was designed to connect United States Department of Defense computers so that communications could be maintained in the event of a nuclear war. Eventually, a number of universities joined the network so that educators and researchers could easily communicate at long distances. Now that the Internet is no longer the sole domain of that early elite, it has become a tool for the people of the world to use as they see fit.

If you had a time machine and could back to use the Internet of the early 1990s, for example, you wouldn't even recognize it as being related to the Internet of today. There were no graphical Web pages and no links that you could click — if you wanted to do anything you had to type in a bunch of esoteric commands and hope for the best. In fact, what most people today think of as being the Internet — the World Wide Web — didn't even exist until the mid-1990s!

The World Wide Web

The World Wide Web — generally called the Web — is the part of the Internet that virtually everyone uses today. The Web is made up of *Web pages* and *Web sites* — groups of related Web pages. Web pages are documents that are located on a computer that is connected to the Internet. These documents are connected by *links* that are really nothing more than the location of documents. In a sense, the Internet could be called a huge interconnected library that enables anyone to be one of the content contributors.

Understanding What You Need

Getting on the Internet has become a whole lot easier in the past few years. Usually, you need a few resources for Internet access from your home:

- A computer or a Web terminal.

- A *Web browser* — software that displays Web pages. In Windows 98, a Web browser — Internet Explorer — is built in, but you can choose a different browser, such as Netscape Navigator or Opera if you prefer.

- An account with an *Internet service provider* — or ISP.

- Information about your Internet account — such as your *user name, password,* and *e-mail address.*

- A *modem* and a phone line (or some other means of physically connecting to the Internet).

If you expect to get Internet access through a network in your office building or school building, you probably won't use a modem. Let your network administrator set up your Internet access.

If your company doesn't have Internet access over a network, don't assume you can unplug an office telephone and connect a modem for dial-up Internet access. Some business phone systems are incompatible with standard modems. In fact, you can damage your equipment if you connect a standard modem to some business phone lines. Check with your company's phone administrator first.

Setting Up Your Account

Because your PC and your phone company probably supply everything else you need to connect to the Internet, here's what you need to do to set up an account with an ISP.

Finding an ISP

The first thing you must do is choose your ISP. When choosing an ISP, here are some things to consider:

- Make certain that you don't have to place a long distance call to connect to the Internet.

- Try to find an ISP that provides access to the Internet and e-mail services that use standard, nonproprietary Internet *protocols*. This enables you to use your choice of programs rather than only the one provided by the ISP. For example, both AOL and CompuServe use proprietary e-mail systems that don't fully support Internet standards.

- Consider whether you'll ever want to access the Internet when traveling. A local ISP may offer advantages, but you won't be able to access your e-mail without making a long distance call if you're on a trip out of your local area.

- You should ask other people in your area which ISPs they use and whether they're satisfied. If everyone is complaining that they always get busy signals or get bumped off the Internet frequently, that's a good sign of an ISP you may wish to avoid.

You can probably find at least one ISP in the Yellow Pages listed under the Internet category. You can also find out which national ISPs serve your area by using the *Connect to the Internet* icon on your Windows 98 desktop. If you don't find that icon, look on your Start menu for the Internet Explorer menu. You should find the Internet Connection Wizard as one of the choices.

National ISPs often provide installation software that sets up your account automatically.

Getting your account information

Regardless of the ISP that you choose, you probably have to supply a credit card number to pay for your account. The ISP in turn should supply you with the following information:

- Your *account name* — the name that you enter when you connect to the Internet.

- Your *password* — a string of characters that prevent others from accessing your account.

- The *dial-in* phone number if you use a modem to access the Internet. If there are alternate numbers, you want them, too, so that your PC can try a different number if the main line is busy.

- The name of the *mail server* so that you can send and receive e-mail.

- The *technical support* telephone number so that you know where to call if you need help connecting.

Passwords may be *case-sensitive* — that is, some letters must be capitals, others must be lowercase. Be sure you know the proper way to enter your password.

The ISP may also tell you about any special settings that you may need to make to connect correctly.

Going Online

After you have the basics of getting onto the Internet, it's time to make that connection. The following sections show you how to connect the first time if you've decided to use the Windows 98 Internet Connection Wizard to set up an account, and then later how to connect after you have an active account.

Connecting the first time

If you have decided to try out one of the ISPs that the Internet Connection Wizard finds for you, here are the steps that you need to follow:

1. Double-click (or single-click, if appropriate) the Connect to the Internet icon on your desktop. If this icon doesn't appear on your desktop, click the Start button and choose Programs⇨Internet Explorer⇨Internet Connection Wizard.

2. Select the "I want to sign up and configure my computer for a new Internet account" option.

3. Click the Next button.

4. Enter your telephone area code in the Area code text box and click Next.

5. From the list that appears, choose an ISP and view their service offerings.

6. Click the Next button when you decide to try an ISP.

7. Click the Finish button to confirm your choice. At this point, you need to provide your personal information to complete the online signup process.

Remember

If you decide to use a local ISP rather than one of those suggested by the Internet Connection Wizard, the ISP will probably provide directions to help you set up a *Dial-Up Networking* connection. For more help on Dial-Up Networking, look at Chapter 10.

Connecting after your account is active

After you have your Internet account established and properly configured, you can begin using the Internet. You can use several methods to connect to the Internet — depending on what you want to accomplish:

■ The most straightforward method of connecting is to double-click the Internet Explorer icon on your desktop or to click the Internet Explorer icon in the *Quick Launch toolbar* just to the right of the Start button.

■ With some types of accounts — notably AOL — you may need to click a different icon to connect. For AOL, you would click the AOL icon.

■ If you prefer using the Windows 98 menus, open the Start menu and select Programs⇨Internet Explorer.

You may need to confirm that you wish to connect, to verify the dial-up phone number, your account name, and your password.

If you share your PC with others, you may not want dial-up networking to automatically enter your logon password. If the password is entered automatically, anyone who has access to your PC can log on and pretend to be you.

In most cases, Windows 98 displays a connection icon in the *system tray* next to the clock. This icon has two lights that flash green as data is sent over your phone line. The connect icon disappears when the connection is broken — providing you with a visual clue that your phone line is once again available. Normally, the connection is broken when you close Internet Explorer, but you can also break the connection manually by right-clicking the connection icon and choosing Disconnect.

You can check the current connection speed by holding your mouse pointer over the connection icon for a few seconds.

Visiting Web Sites

Of course, the real reason for setting up your Internet account is so that you can browse Web sites. In the following sections, you learn what you need to know in order to visit those millions of interesting places.

Understanding Internet addresses

Each Web page has a *URL* — Uniform Resource Locator — that uniquely identifies exactly how to locate the page. Those

URLs are really the addresses of each Web page, and they enable your Web browser to find and display the pages that you want to see. Here's a breakdown of how URLs are specified:

```
Protocol://address/subaddress1 . . .
```

The *protocol* is simply an indicator of the type of address that you want to visit. In most cases, Web pages use `http` — Hypertext Transfer Protocol (or `https` if the Web site is on a secure server, such as one that takes credit card orders). Following the protocol is always a colon and two forward slashes (`://`). Next follows the Web site address, such as `www.cliffsnotes.com`. If you want to visit a page that is part of the same Web site, that page address is indicated by a slash and then the page address. In some cases, Web pages may be several levels deep, so several slashes may separate individual sub-addresses. Figure 7-1 shows where the address `http://www.cliffsnotes.com` takes you.

Figure 7-1:   Enter the URL in the Address box to visit a Web site.

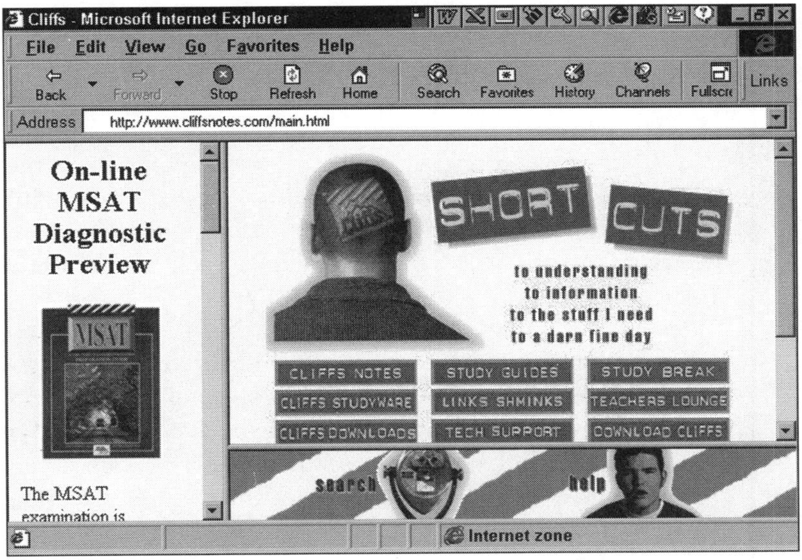

Web site addresses usually don't have true spaces. If you see a Web site address that appears to have a space in the address, the space is almost always filled by an *underscore* (_).

Using links

When you visit Web sites, you generally see a number of *links* — places that you can click to jump to another Web page. Some links are easy to identify because they appear as underlined text that is in a different color than the surrounding text. Other links may appear in the form of buttons or pictures. Whenever your mouse pointer is over a link, the pointer changes from an arrow to a hand.

You'll probably discover that some links are *broken*. If you receive a message telling you that the address cannot be located or that the server is not responding, you won't be able to visit the page that the link points to — at least not right now. Sometimes, links appear broken if the computer that hosts the Web page is temporarily unavailable. You can try again later and you may be able to view the page.

Saving your favorite sites

Typing the same URL every time you want to visit the same Web page again can get old pretty fast. You can make the process a whole lot easier by saving the address in your list of favorite Web sites. After you do, you can simply choose the site from your list, and Internet Explorer takes you directly to that site.

You can easily add a Web site to your list of favorites. Simply choose Favorites⇨Add to Favorites to display the Add Favorite dialog box, as shown in Figure 7-2. You can also right-click a link on the current Web page and choose Add to Favorites from the pop-up context menu to save the link to your favorites list.

Figure 7-2:   Save Web sites in your list of favorites so that you can easily return for a future visit.

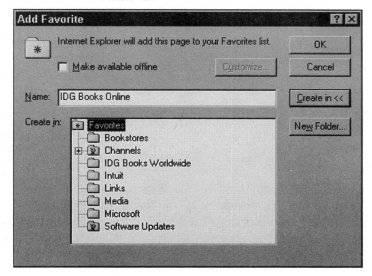

If a Web page contains several links that you want to add to your favorites, save the Web page in favorites rather than each individual link to reduce the size of your favorites list.

You may wish to create folders to help organize your favorites. When the Add Favorite dialog box is open, click the Create in button to expand the dialog box. Then you can choose one of the existing folders or click the New Folder button and create a folder.

When you save your favorite Web sites, you may want to modify the default name that Internet Explorer offers for the site to make the name more descriptive.

After you save your favorite Web sites, you can quickly return to those sites by choosing them from one of your Favorites lists. If you're already online, click the Favorites menu and choose from the list. If you aren't online, click the Start button and choose the site from the Favorites menu.

Using the Address toolbar

Unless you click one of your favorites on the Favorites menu, Internet Explorer automatically loads a *start page* every time you start Internet Explorer. You can bypass this start page by using the following handy trick:

1. Right-click the Windows 98 taskbar.

2. Choose Toolbars⇨Address from the pop-up context menu.

3. Type the URL in the Address box and press Enter.

You can also type URLs in the Windows Explorer Address box. Either way, Internet Explorer loads, makes the connection to the Internet, and goes directly to the page you specify.

Sending links and pages

As you browse the Internet, you're bound to come across interesting Web pages that you just have to share with someone else. Here are a couple of ways you can send a Web page or link to someone:

■ While you're visiting the page, choose File⇨Send⇨Page by E-mail to send a copy of the page as it currently exists. This option is best if something important is currently on the page and the page is likely to change.

■ If you're visiting a page that is interesting but you'd rather the recipient visit the page and see the latest information, choose File⇨Send⇨Link by E-mail. Not only is a link much quicker and smaller to send, but the recipient of your message won't be viewing an out-of-date page.

■ If you're not currently viewing the page, type the URL in an e-mail message or copy the URL from your \Windows\Favorites folder.

Using the History list

If you save every page that you visit in your Favorites list, the list would soon grow so large that it would be virtually unusable. Still, you may want to return to a page that you visited even if it isn't on the Favorites list.

Internet Explorer maintains a *History list* that contains a link to each page you visit. By opening this list, you can find links — organized by Web site — to each page you visited on any particular day. When you find a page you want to visit again, just click the link and Internet Explorer takes you to that page.

You can view the History list by clicking the History icon — the icon that looks like a sundial — or by selecting View⇨Explorer Bar⇨History. Figure 7-3 shows how your History list might look if you visit several pages at www.idgbooks.com in a day.

Figure 7-3:   Use the History list to revisit interesting pages that you didn't save in Favorites.

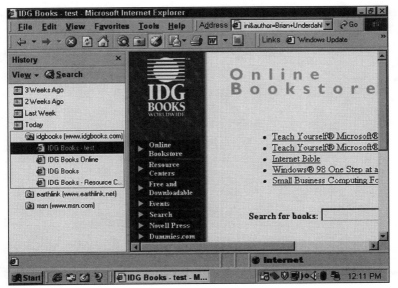

You can set the number of days that items remain in your History list by choosing View⟹Internet Options (in Internet Explorer 4) or Tools⟹Internet Options (in Internet Explorer 5). Then use the History options near the bottom of the General tab to set the number of days or to clear the History list.

Finding Things Online

To use a search engine to find information, you can go directly to the search engine's Web site — such as www.yahoo.com — or you can use the Internet Explorer Search Explorer Bar. To display the Search Explorer Bar, click the Search button on the Internet Explorer toolbar or select View⟹Explorer Bar⟹Search.

CHAPTER 8

ADDING AND REMOVING PROGRAMS

One of the greatest things about PCs is that they aren't limited to performing one single task. If you load the right software, you can have your computer do hundreds of very different things. Buying new programs isn't the only way to enhance your PC. You'll probably be at least a little surprised when you find out how many additional pieces of Windows 98 itself are available right on your Windows 98 CD-ROM.

In this chapter, you learn how to install new programs, how to add additional pieces of Windows 98, where you can find the free Windows 98 Resource Kit Sampler, and how to get rid of junk that's just wasting disk space.

Installing More Programs

Installing a new program on your Windows 98-based PC isn't quite the simple task that you may expect. You may expect that installing a new program would be pretty straightforward. The reality, however, is just a little different.

Adding programs

Installing a new program in Windows 98 is pretty easy. Follow these steps:

1. Insert the new program's installation CD-ROM into your CD-ROM drive. If the installation program starts automatically, skip to Step 7.

2. If the installation program doesn't run automatically, click the Start button and choose Settings⇨Control Panel.

3. When the Control Panel opens, double-click the Add/Remove Programs icon.

4. In the Add/Remove Programs Properties dialog box that appears, click the Install button on the Install/Uninstall tab.

5. Click the Next button to have Windows 98 search for the install program.

6. If the correct program is shown, click the Finish button. If the installation instructions indicate that you should enter a different command than the one shown, do so before you click Finish.

7. Follow the on-screen prompts to complete the installation.

You should have a choice of where you want the program installed, as well as a choice of where the program appears on your Start menu. Depending on the program that you're installing, you may need to enter a serial number and you may need to select which components to install.

If you want to decide which components to install, select an installation option — such as Custom — rather than Default.

Because installing new programs may cause existing programs to fail to work properly, you may want to run each of your important programs as soon as possible to verify that they still work. That way, if you have problems, you have a good clue about the cause.

Sharing files

Windows 98 programs often share a number of files. When you install a program that uses a shared file, the installation program is supposed to check to see if the shared file is already installed. If it is, the installation program is only supposed to add its own version of the file if the current version is older. Unfortunately, this scheme sometimes breaks down in the real world. Programmers may decide to bypass the version check for what seems (to them, anyway) very practical reasons — they know that their programs run correctly on the version of the shared file that they' are installing. If you have a problem, it won't be their program that malfunctions, so you probably won't call them for support.

If some of your existing programs start having problems after you've installed a new program, it's almost always the fault of the new program. Try reinstalling the old programs to see if the problems go away. If that doesn't help, it's time to call for help.

Adding More Windows Features

Did you realize that quite a few bits and pieces of Windows 98 haven't been installed? When Windows 98 is installed on a PC, the typical components are installed but a number of others aren't.

On the other hand, some Windows 98 components already installed on your system may be of no use to you. You can remove them and recover the otherwise wasted disk space.

Figure 8-1 shows the Windows Setup tab of the Add/Remove Programs Properties dialog box. You use this tab to select the optional Windows 98 components that you would like to install or remove. Click the Start button, choose Settings⇨Control Panel, and then open Add/Remove Programs to display this dialog box. Click the Windows Setup tab.

Figure 8-1:   Choose the optional Windows 98 components that you want installed.

You see a number of different categories of optional components. Each category includes a number of individual items that you can view and select by first selecting the category and then clicking the Details button. Add a check in front of any item that you want installed, and remove the check to uninstall items.

Browse through each component category to view the descriptions of the individual components.

After you make all your choices, click the Apply button to add and remove the optional components. You may need to insert your Windows 98 CD-ROM. When the installation is complete, close the dialog box and restart your system.

Adding the Windows Resource Kit

Your Windows 98 CD-ROM includes some additional components that don't appear anywhere on the Add/Remove Programs Properties dialog box's Windows Setup tab. The most important of these is probably the Windows 98 Resource Kit Sampler, which is a collection of useful utility programs. For example, Tweakui, one of the programs in the sampler, enables you to fine-tune your PC in ways you never thought possible. Installing this program adds the Tweakui icon to your Control Panel.

To install most of the components of the Windows 98 Resource Kit Sampler, follow these steps:

1. Insert your Windows 98 CD-ROM into your CD-ROM drive.

2. If the Windows 98 CD-ROM automatically starts, click Browse this CD. If the CD-ROM doesn't start automatically, open Windows Explorer and choose your CD-ROM drive.

3. Open the \tools\reskit folder.

4. Double-click (or single-click depending on your system setup) Setup.exe to begin the installation.

5. View Readme.doc to view additional information about the Resource Kit.

Some Resource Kit utilities are very powerful tools. Before using these tools, make certain that you view the help files so that you don't accidentally damage your system.

Removing Programs

An old computer truism says that data expands to fill the available space. Removing a single program can free up more disk space than is used by hundreds of document files.

Before you remove an old program, make certain that you really don't need the program. If you used the program to create document files, you wouldn't want to remove the program only to find that no other program could open those files. Also make certain that you still have the original installation disks so that you can reinstall a program if necessary.

Here's how you uninstall most programs:

1. Choose Start⇨Settings⇨Control Panel.

2. Open the Add/Remove Programs item.

3. Select the program you want to uninstall from the list in the bottom section of the Install/Uninstall tab of the Add/Remove Programs Properties dialog box.

4. Click the Add/Remove button.

5. Follow the on-screen directions.

CHAPTER 9
PLAYING SOUND AND VIDEO

IN THIS CHAPTER

- Understanding multimedia
- Playing multimedia files
- Adding sounds to events
- Controlling the volume
- Recording your own sounds

Modern PCs are anything but boring. *Multimedia* — sights and sounds — has made the PC a very entertaining piece of electronic hardware. In this chapter, you learn the basics of using multimedia content on your computer.

Multimedia in a Nutshell

On the PC, multimedia generally refers to content that is dynamic rather than static — or more simply, audio and sometimes video. You can, for example, use sounds to tell you when something happens on your PC — such as when a new e-mail message arrives.

Understanding sound

Sound files are document files that tell your PC how to generate various types of sounds. Windows 98 primarily uses two types of sound files:

■ *WAV files* are recorded sounds. These sounds can include any type of sound that you can record — music, voices, sound effects, and so on. WAV files get their name from their most common file extension, WAV.

■ *MIDI files* are instructions that tell your computer how to generate sounds. MIDI stands for *Musical Instrument Digital Interface*. MIDI files typically have an MID file extension.

Because WAV files are recorded sounds, they tend to sound the same on all PCs. MIDI files can sound considerably different depending on the capabilities of your sound card.

Voices that play on your PC are always WAV files.

Understanding video

Video files are typically document files that contain a recorded video portion along with a synchronized audio portion.

In most cases, video files that are intended for playback on a PC are best displayed in a relatively small window rather than full-screen. Some types of video files — notably MPEG files — use *data compression* to pack more multimedia content into a given amount of space.

Running Multimedia Files

Playing multimedia files used to be a lot more difficult than it is today. After you located the files that you want to play, you had to make certain that you had the right program to play that particular type of file.

Playing computer sounds and videos

Windows 98 comes with a very capable multimedia player — the Windows Media Player shown in Figure 9-1. The current version of this player can handle at least 24 different types of multimedia files.

Figure 9-1: The Windows Media Player can play many different types of multimedia files.

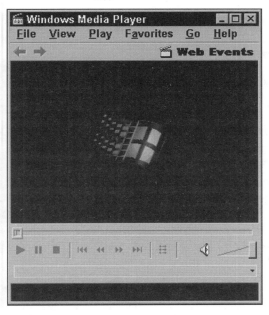

If your Windows Media Player doesn't look like the figure, use the Windows Update feature on the Start menu to download a newer version.

You can use several different methods to play multimedia files with the Windows Media Player, depending on your needs:

■ You can open the Start menu and select Programs⇨Accessories⇨Entertainment⇨Windows Media Player and then choose File⇨Open to select files to play.

■ If the Windows Media Player is already open, you can drag and drop multimedia files onto the Windows Media Player window to play those files.

■ You can double-click a multimedia file in Windows Explorer or on your desktop to open the file and play it using Windows Media Player.

Listening to music CDs

Your PC can also play audio CDs in your CD-ROM drive. Depending on how your system is configured, all that may be necessary to play an audio CD is to insert it into your CD-ROM drive. If *AutoPlay* is enabled for the CD-ROM drive, the Windows CD Player starts up and plays the CD. If AutoPlay is not enabled, you can start the CD Player by selecting Programs⇨Accessories⇨Entertainment⇨CD Player from the Start menu.

The CD Player has controls that are like those you would find on a standard CD player. You can play the CD, skip to a different track, or even play the tracks randomly.

If you play a lot of audio CDs on your PC, you may want to consider adding the Plus! 98 upgrade to your system. This upgrade includes the Deluxe CD Player, which can download all the information about most audio CDs from the Internet. When you insert a new audio CD, the Deluxe CD Player quickly finds the CD name, the artist, and all the track names and stores that information in a database on your PC.

Making Sounds Automatic

In addition to simply opening and playing multimedia files manually, Windows 98 also enables you to attach sounds to events. In the following sections, you learn how to add the sounds that you want to events.

Adding computer system sounds

Windows 98 has a list of *system events* — things that happen on your computer — that can have sounds associated with them. Some programs add their own events to this list.

The sounds that you can attach to events are WAV sounds — recorded sounds. As you learn later in this chapter in the section "Recording Your Own Sounds," you can create sounds that you can add to events.

To add sounds to system events, follow these steps:

1. Choose Start⇨Settings⇨Control Panel.

2. Double-click the Sounds icon in the Control Panel to open the Sounds Properties dialog box, as shown in Figure 9-2.

3. Click one of the events that has a sound — look for the speaker icon in front of events with sounds — and click the Play button.

4. Select an event and click the Browse button to look for a sound file to attach to the event.

5. Click OK to return to the Sounds Properties dialog box.

6. If you wish to save different sound schemes, use the Save As button to name each scheme.

7. Click OK to close the dialog box.

Figure 9-2: The Sounds Properties dialog box enables you to add sounds to events.

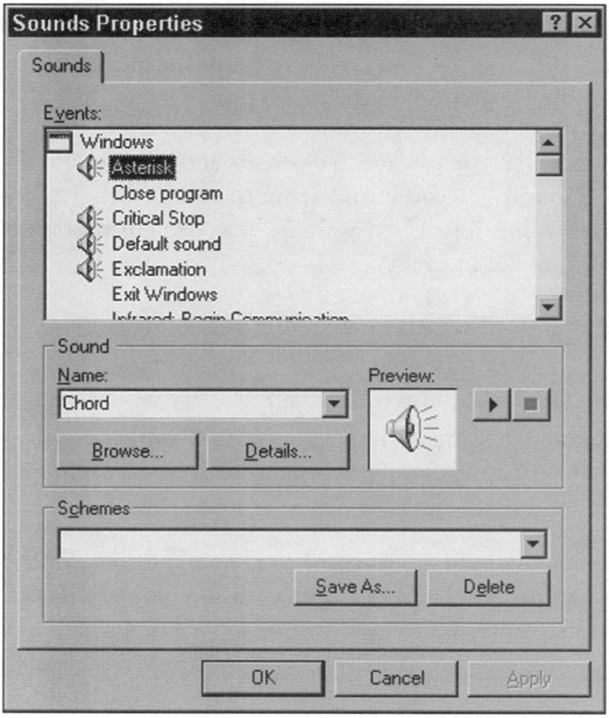

Sounds Properties

Sounds

Events:

- Windows
  - Asterisk
  - Close program
  - Critical Stop
  - Default sound
  - Exclamation
  - Exit Windows
  - Infrared: Begin Communication

Sound

Name:
Chord

Preview:

Browse...   Details...

Schemes

Save As...   Delete

OK   Cancel   Apply

Attaching sounds to documents

You can also add sounds to your documents. If you find an
Insert menu in a program, use the Insert⇨File command to
add a sound file to the document. You can also use the drag
and drop technique to add a sound file to most documents.

Sound files attached to documents are only useful if the document recipient can play the file. Don't bother attaching
sound files unless the document will be viewed on a computer.

Controlling the Volume

The sounds that you play on your PC's speakers probably have a wide range of volume levels. To adjust the volume you can turn to the Windows 98 volume control.

Adjusting volume

If you look at the *system tray* — the array of icons next to the time display in the Windows 98 taskbar — you notice one icon that looks like a speaker. This is the volume control icon.

To adjust the overall volume level, click the volume control icon, which displays the master volume control slider that you can drag up or down to adjust the volume.

You can also use this control to quickly disable all sounds. Just click the volume icon and then select the Mute check box.

Balancing sound sources

Several different sound sources are likely on your PC. All these different sources probably won't supply sound at the same volume level. Fortunately, you have an easy solution to this problem — the full volume control.

To display the full volume control, double-click the system tray speaker icon. The full volume control includes separate controls for each sound source so that you can adjust each of them for an optimum mix. The full volume control also has balance sliders to adjust the right/left speaker balance. You find a Mute check box for each sound source so that you can silence any one source individually.

Clicking the Mute check boxes may prevent you from hearing a sound source through your speakers, but it may not prevent that sound source from appearing in a sound that you record. Be sure to move the slider to the minimum volume level for any source you don't want to record before you begin recording sounds.

Customizing the volume control panel

The controls that appear on the full volume control are generally the ones that are most important for playing back sounds. You can add or remove individual controls by selecting Options⤳Properties and then choosing which controls you want to see.

Recording Your Own Sounds

Because WAV files are simply recorded sounds, you can create your own sound files from almost any source that plays sound through your PC sound card. If you have a microphone attached to your system, you can even record your own voice messages.

Although you can record sounds from virtually any sound source, remember that commercially produced materials are covered by copyrights.

Using the Sound Recorder

The *Sound Recorder* is a Windows 98 accessory that enables you to record your own WAV files. To open the Sound Recorder, click the Start button and then select Programs⤳Accessories⤳Entertainment⤳Sound Recorder.

Before you begin recording, open the full volume control. The microphone input is generally muted by default, which can cause a lot of frustration when you try to make a recording because your message won't be recorded.

To record a message, click the Record button and begin speaking. As you record, the small window in the center of the Sound Recorder shows the differences in volume level. If the line stays flat, it's a good indication that your sound source volume level is too low.

After you finish recording, click the Stop button. Then use the buttons and the slider to play back the recording. Select File⇨Save to keep your recording.

Setting the sound properties

Sound files can be recorded in a number of different quality levels. Higher quality levels sound better, of course, but higher levels generally use considerably more disk space. To choose the recording quality level, follow these steps:

1. Select File⇨Properties.

2. Click the Convert Now button.

3. Choose the quality level that you prefer. Notice that each quality level provides an indication of the size of the sound file.

4. Close the dialog boxes and return to Sound Recorder to use the new settings for your next recording.

Unless you have a strong reason for choosing a format other than the default PCM, you should probably stick with the default format — especially if you intend to share your recording with other people.

CHAPTER 10

FREE WINDOWS ACCESSORIES

IN THIS CHAPTER

- Using the general purpose accessories
- Using the system tools
- Using the communications accessories

Windows 98 includes a lot of accessories. In this chapter, you have a quick look at a selection of some of the most useful accessories.

I can't tell you everything about the Windows 98 accessory programs in just a few pages. So you may want to treat this chapter as a sampler that shows you what is available.

Although Windows 98 includes several games, I won't cover those in this chapter. You'll probably have no difficulty figuring those out for yourself!

See Chapter 8 for how to add additional Windows 98 programs, including any of the accessory programs that may not be installed by default.

Sampling Windows Programs

The general purpose accessories are relatively simple programs that you may use on a regular basis. You find each program on the Programs⇨Accessories group on your Start menu.

Writing with Notepad

Notepad is a *text editor*. In some ways, a text editor is like a word processing program, but a text editors don't perform any formatting — which can be important because some files must be plain text without any special characters.

Windows 98 uses a number of files that must be plain text without any formatting. These include the following:

■ *MS-DOS batch files* — command files, such as AUTOEXEC.BAT, that are used to perform tasks at the MS-DOS command prompt

■ *Configuration files* — special files that hold settings that enable your hardware and software to function correctly on your system

■ *Log files* — files that contain the results of certain operations, such as program installations or the errors encountered while attempting to perform tasks

You may occasionally see a message that tells you that a file is too large to be opened in Notepad. This message then asks if you wish to open the file in WordPad. It's okay to do so, but make certain that you only save any changes in the plain-text format to avoid problems with the file.

The printing process is the same in most Windows programs. Check out Chapter 11 to print out a copy of your text.

Writing with WordPad

WordPad can work with plain-text files, but it can also open and save Word-format files. WordPad can also apply formatting to your documents. WordPad doesn't, however, include tools like a spell checker.

If you don't have Microsoft Word installed on your system, you can use WordPad to open any Word documents that someone sends you.

Because WordPad doesn't run any Word macros, you can safely open any Word document in WordPad without worrying about macro viruses.

Drawing pictures

Paint is a *bitmap editor* — a program that you can use to create and edit bitmap images. *Bitmaps* are graphic images that use small individual blocks — *pixels* — to form a picture. Paint can work with several different image formats. The default Paint format is the Windows Bitmap (BMP) format, but Paint can also open and edit JPEG and GIF images — the two image formats that are most common on the Web.

Paint has a series of tools in a tool palette along the left edge of the Paint window. Along the bottom of the window, you see a set of color selection boxes. You use these tools and color selection palettes to create or modify images much the same way you might use cans of spray paint or colored pens to paint a picture.

If you use an image as the background for your Windows 98 desktop, you can modify that image in Paint.

Scanning images

Imaging is a graphics program that is focused on acquiring images from scanners and on adding annotations to existing images.

Imaging enables you to have several images open at the same time. This makes Imaging adept at handling multiple page faxes.

When you're working with multiple page documents in Imaging, you may want to click the Page and Thumbnails View button to display each page of the document using a small thumbnail view and the currently selected page in a normal-sized view. To switch to a different page, you can simply click the thumbnail of the page you want to view.

Calculating

Calculator is a program that serves as a handy on-screen memory calculator. With both standard and scientific modes, Calculator is useful for both simple calculations and much more complex ones. When you open Calculator, you can use the View menu to switch between the standard and scientific modes.

To use Calculator, you can enter numbers using the number keys on your keyboard or by clicking the buttons on Calculator itself. You need to click the buttons to use most of the functions.

Figure 10-1 shows Calculator in scientific mode. In this figure, the pi button was clicked to demonstrate the precision that is available.

Housekeeping

The system tools are Windows 98 accessories that generally perform tasks that are important to keeping your system running efficiently. You can access these tools by choosing Start⇨Programs⇨Accessories⇨System Tools.

Figure 10-1: Calculator can perform sophisticated calculations that would require an expensive hand-held calculator.

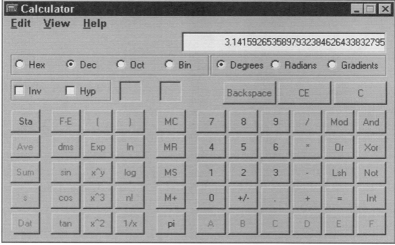

Archiving your files

Backup is a program that you use to make safe copies of your important files so that you can easily recover from hardware errors and user errors.

When you use Backup, you can choose specific files and folders that you want to save, which is important because a partial backup that saves your data files is really all that you need, and a partial backup takes far less time than a full backup of everything on your system. After you set up a list of files and folders to back up, you can save that list as a *backup set* to use in future backups.

If your PC has a tape backup drive, Backup uses the tape drive for backups. Most tapes have fairly high capacity, so you can typically start a backup and walk away.

Always maintain at least two sets of backup disks or tapes and alternate their use. This practice protects you in the event one set of disks or tapes becomes damaged.

Maintaining your disks

Several Windows 98 accessories fall into the category of disk tools. These tools help you maintain the health of your disk drives. Here is a brief description of each tool:

■ *DriveSpace* is a tool that compresses the data on your disks, which makes your disk drives seem larger because more data can be stored in less space.

■ *Compression Agent* is a tool that works with DriveSpace to squeeze out a bit more room on compressed drives.

■ *Disk Cleanup* is a tool that removes unneeded files from your hard disk to free up the space that they're wasting.

■ *Disk Defragmenter* is a tool that makes your hard disk more efficient by rearranging your files. Defragmenting makes reading your files more efficient and improves the performance of your system.

■ *ScanDisk* is a tool that looks for and corrects trouble on your disk drives.

Scheduling tasks

Certain tasks — such as disk maintenance — are extremely important if you want your PC to keep running at its best. Windows 98 can help by running those tasks automatically on a regular schedule.

Windows 98 includes two tools that make scheduling routine maintenance at lot easier. The *Task Scheduler* (which appears as Scheduled Tasks on the Start menu) automatically runs programs at specified times. The *Maintenance Wizard* helps you create routine maintenance tasks within the Task Scheduler.

You can view the current task schedule by double-clicking the Task Scheduler icon in the system tray. When the Task Scheduler is open, you can also create new tasks or modify the schedule for existing ones.

The Maintenance Wizard schedules tasks that can make your PC run more efficiently. You can choose to use an express or a custom mode to schedule these tasks. Express mode is somewhat easier, of course, but it doesn't give you as much control or information as the custom mode does.

If you add Plus! 98 to your system, the Maintenance Wizard can add some additional tasks, including automatic virus scans.

Finding system information

The System Information tool is actually several important tools in one. As Figure 10-2 shows, System Information has a Tools menu that provides access to a number of programs that you can use to diagnose and correct problems that you may encounter.

System Information provides a wealth of detail about your PC. It shows you information about your hardware, the software that is running, and any drivers that may be loaded.

Although the Tools menu has a number of interesting looking tools, remember that you could damage your system by "playing around" with these tools. You can, as an example, make configuration changes that could prevent Windows 98 from starting.

Figure 10-2: The System Information tool includes a number of high-powered options.

The Hardware Resources branch contains a high level of detail about the various system resources, such as *IRQs, DMA channels,* and *I/O addresses.* You can use the Copy button to copy this information to the Windows 98 clipboard and then paste it into an e-mail message to a technical support person if your troubleshooting becomes particularly difficult.

Click the Print button to print out the currently displayed System Information branch.

Inserting special characters

Character Map is a tool that enables you to easily insert special characters into your documents.

When you open Character Map, you see all the available characters in the currently selected font. If you want to enter a symbol rather than a normal character, select a symbol font, such as Symbol or Wingdings.

After you click a character, use the arrow keys to move the magnifier through the character set.

You can copy characters to the Character Map scratchpad by double-clicking the character or by clicking the Select button. When you have copied all the characters you need, click the Copy button so that you can close Character Map and copy the characters into your document.

Don't change the font of the characters that you've copied into your document. Changing the font may result in a different character being displayed.

Communicating

Windows 98 has several communications tools on the Programs⇨Accessories⇨Communications section of the Start menu.

Connecting through Dial-up Networking

Dial-up Networking is essential for connecting to the Internet, but that isn't its only purpose. As the name implies, you use Dial-up Networking to establish a remote connection to a network — often through a modem.

When you set up an account with an Internet service provider, Windows 98 creates a Dial-up Networking connection that contains all the parameters necessary to successfully establish that connection, as shown in Figure 10-3.

When you open the Dial-up Networking folder, you see icons for each of your current connections. You can establish the connection by double-clicking the appropriate connection icon. If you wish to modify the properties for a connection, right-click the connection icon and choose Properties from the pop-up context menu.

Figure 10-3:   Use the Dial-Up Networking folder to create connections to the Internet
and other computers.

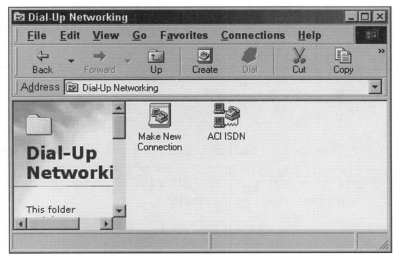

NetMeeting works far better if each participant has a high-
speed connection to the Internet, such as ISDN and DSL.

Sharing files through Direct Cable Connection

If you have two PCs, you probably have the need to share
files between those systems on occasion. Direct Cable Connection uses either a serial or a parallel cable to connect two
PCs directly so that they can share files.

CHAPTER 11

PRINTING

IN THIS CHAPTER

- Installing printer drivers
- Printing

The paperless office has yet to arrive. And until it does, you're probably going to want to print some of those wonderful documents that you create. This chapter explains how you get your printer ready to print.

Printing

The easy, no-nonsense way to print in most Windows programs is to use the Print button — the one with the picture of a printer — on the toolbar. Clicking this button usually results in printing one copy of the current document to the default printer, using the default printer settings.

If you want more control over the way a document prints — which printer it prints to, the number of copies, and so on — choose File➪Print to bring up the Print dialog box (see Figure 11-1).

Warning

If your Windows 98 system doesn't have the necessary *printer drivers* installed for your printer, you need to install the drivers before you can print. If the printer you want to use can be selected in the Name option on the Print dialog box, someone probably has installed the driver for you. Driver installation is covered later in this chapter.

Figure 11-1: The Print dialog box controls your printer every time you print.

Print

Printer

Name: NEC SuperScript 860 ▼   Properties

Status: Default printer; Ready
Type: NEC SuperScript 860
Where: LPT1:
Comment: ☐ Print to file

Print range   Copies

○ All   Number of copies: 1 ⊞
○ Pages from: 1 to:
○ Selection   [1][2][3] ☐ Collate

                                OK   Cancel

Before you print your document, use Print Preview to make sure your document will print the way you want it to. Print Preview can save you money on ink cartridges and paper. Just click the Print Preview button on the toolbar — the one with the paper and magnifying glass — or choose File⇨Print Preview.

The Print dialog box

The Print dialog box has a variety of options for you to play around with, depending on the program you're printing from. Check these out:

■ To print to a printer other than the default, click the down arrow next to the Name box and select a printer.

■ To change the number of copies you want to print, use the arrows next to Number of copies. You can also type in the number of copies you want.

■ To change which pages you want to print, choose from the options in the Page Range area.

■ If you're printing more that one copy of a multi-page document, click the Collate check box to save yourself a lot of sorting and collating time.

Click OK in the Print dialog box to print your document with your new settings.

The Page Setup dialog box

You can access additional printer settings from the Page Setup dialog box. Just choose File➪Page Setup to call up the Page Setup dialog box. The changes you make in this dialog box remain in effect until you change them again.

Remember

The following options vary depending on your printer and the program that you're printing from.

■ To print on different sized paper, click the down arrow next to the Size box and choose a new paper size. Make sure that the size you choose matches the paper that you loaded into your printer.

■ To switch between multiple paper sources, select which one to use from the Source drop-down list. This option is especially handy if you have a printer with plain paper in one tray and letterhead paper in another.

■ To change the page orientation, choose either landscape or portrait. Portrait orientation is what you're used to — the shorter edge of the paper is at the top and bottom. Landscape turns the paper on its side — the longer edge is on the top and bottom. Use landscape for documents that are too wide to fit on a portrait-oriented page.

■ To change how much blank space is between the edge of the paper and the text of the document, type new values in the Top, Bottom, Left, or Right boxes of the Margins area.

Installing Printer Drivers

Before you can print to a printer, you must properly connect it to the computer. You also have to make sure that your computer and the printer speak the same language. You accomplish this by installing a piece of software known as a printer driver. A *printer driver* is a set of instructions that tells Windows how to access the printer's functions. Every printer should come with a printer driver created by the printer's manufacturer.

Here's how you introduce your computer to your printer. Make sure that you have your Windows CD handy when performing the following steps. If a CD is included with your printer, you need that CD, too.

1. Choose Start⇨Settings⇨Printers. The Printers window appears with an icon for each printer installed on your computer, as shown in Figure 11-2.

2. Double-click the Add Printer icon to start the Add Printer Wizard.

3. Click Next.

4. Select Local printer to tell Windows that the printer is attached to your computer.

5. Click Next.

6. Select the company that made your printer from the Manufacturers list, and then select the correct model of your printer from the Printers list.

Figure 11-2: The Printers icons allow you to control printers connected to your computer.

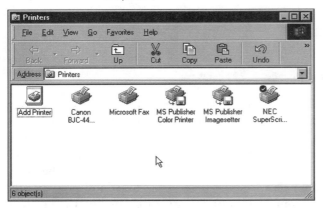

7. Click Next.

8. Select the LPT1: option to tell Windows that the printer is connected to your printer port.

9. Click Next.

10. Type a name for your printer or accept the default name. If you plan to use this printer most often, click Yes to set it as your default printer. If you have more than one printer and this printer won't be the primary printer, click No.

11. Click Next.

12. Click Yes and then click Finish to have Windows print a test page. If Windows can't find the required files on your hard disk, Windows asks you to place your Windows CD in the CD-ROM drive. Click OK after you have done so.

13. After Windows prints the test page, click Yes if the page printed successfully.

14. Click the Close button in the upper-right corner of the printer window. Now you're all set to print!

CLIFFSNOTES REVIEW

Use this CliffsNotes Review to practice what you've learned in this book and to build your confidence in doing the job right the first time. After you work through the review questions, the problem-solving exercises, and the fun and useful practice projects, you're well on your way to achieving your goal of using Windows 98 confidently.

Q&A

1. How should you exit from an application that's running?

    a. Push the Reset button.

    b. Save your work and then close the program.

    c. Click the lower-left corner of your screen.

    d. Turn the computer off.

2. What happens when you click a menu name?

    a. Nothing; you have to use the keyboard to use menus.

    b. A menu that's open on-screen closes.

    c. A menu appears, showing commands you can click.

    d. b. and c.

3. How do you start a program?

    a. Use the mouse to highlight its name and then press Enter.

    b. Find the program in your computer's directory of folders and double-click its name.

    c. Type the program's name at the command prompt and press Enter.

    d. All of the above.

4. What happens first when your computer boots up?

    a. A built-in program starts the operating system.

    b. Your user interface appears on the screen.

    c. The computer prints out a test document.

    d. The document you're working on appears.

5 How often should you save your work?

   a. Every ten to fifteen minutes.

   b. Every two or three hours.

   c. Weekly.

   d. Never; computers are completely reliable.

6. What is a boot disk?

   a. A disk that comes in a hard plastic case.

   b. A disk that contains startup files for emergency use.

   c. A disk you must always put in the drive after you boot up.

   d. A disk that contains user's instructions for your system.

7. Which of these methods can you use to transfer files from the C: drive to a floppy-disk drive labeled B:?

   a. From drive C:, select the files you want and then double-click the first one.

   b. Open a window for each drive, select files in the drive C: window, press and hold down the left mouse button, move the mouse pointer over to the drive B: window, and release.

   c. Open a window for the B: drive, use the mouse to select files in the drive C: window, and then type **copy these files to B:**.

   d. Write down the names of the files you want to copy, close the user interface, reboot the computer, and then type **copy to B:** at the command prompt, followed by the file names.

8. How can you determine whether an application is appropriate to run on your PC?

   a. Read about it in a computer magazine.

   b. Check the system requirements on the software box.

   c. Know which peripherals are installed in your system.

   d. All of the above.

9. What is the best approach to buying a PC?

   a. See it advertised on TV at a great price, and go buy it.

   b. Buy as many features and devices as you can afford.

c. Always buy state-of-the-art and upgrade every 6 months.

d. Decide what you want to use a PC for, find the software that will do it, and look for a PC that runs the software well.

Answers: (1) b. (2) d. (3) d. (4) 1. (5) 1. (6) b. (7) b. (8) d. (9).

Scenarios

(1) You finished a letter to a friend and saved it, but when you open your word processor, you can't find it. How can you find your letter?

_____

_____

(2) You bring home a new laser printer for your computer and connect it to your system, but when you try to print a document, nothing happens. What can you do to fix the problem?

_____

_____

Answers: (1) Use your computer's file-management utility program (such as Windows Explorer or File Manager) to show you the directory tree; use the utility's Search (or similar) command to hunt for the file name of your letter; when you find the letter, save it to a specific folder (most Windows users can use the My Documents folder). (2) Make sure the correct device driver for your printer is installed; the printer should include a disk that has the driver program and instructions that tell you how to install it.

Visual Test

Which of the ports in back of your computer connect it to the printer, the monitor, the mouse, and the Internet? Sketch them and check your cables to make sure they are correct for each port.

Consider This

What tasks are you doing now that would go faster and easier on a computer? Which tasks are easier if you use pen and paper? What kind of work is best suited to a computer?

Practice Project

Use your word processor to create your résumé and give it a professional look:

1. Start your word processor.

2. Start a new document in your word processor.

3. Place a clean copy of your old résumé on a copy stand next to your screen.

4. Type the text of your résumé into your on-screen document.

5. Use your word processor's paragraph-formatting commands to left-align your résumé list items and to center-align your section headings.

6. To preserve the work you've done so far, save your document with the title **myresume.doc**.

7. Use your mouse or keyboard to select the entire document, and then use your word processor's character-formatting commands to select a businesslike font for your résumé.

8. Spell-check your résumé and edit it for grammar and accuracy.

9. Save your résumé twice more — once to a directory on your hard drive (most Windows users can use the My Documents directory), and once to a formatted floppy disk so that you have a backup copy. Then print out and file the updated résumé.

CLIFFSNOTES RESOURCE CENTER

The learning doesn't need to stop here. CliffsNotes Resource Center shows you the best of the best — links to the best information in print and online about Windows 98. Look for these terrific resources at your favorite bookstore or local library and on the Internet. When you're online, make your first stop www.cliffsnotes.com, where you can find even more incredibly useful information about Windows 98.

Books

This CliffsNotes book is one of many great books for PC users from IDG Books Worldwide, Inc. So if you want some great next-step books, check out these other publications:

Windows 98 Bible, by Alan Simpson, is a full-featured reference that includes a CD-ROM full of software tools. IDG Books Worldwide, Inc., $39.99.

PC Upgrade and Repair Simplified, by Ruth Maran, is a guide to maintaining and improving your PC. IDG Books Worldwide, Inc., $24.99.

You can easily find books published by IDG Books Worldwide, Inc., in your favorite bookstores, at the library, on the Internet, and at a store near you. We also have three Web sites that you can use to read about all the books we publish:

www.cliffsnotes.com
www.dummies.com
www.idgbooks.com

Internet

Check out these Web resources for more information on Windows 98.

Microsoft Windows Update, `http://window supdate.microsoft.com`, takes you directly to the latest official news from Microsoft about Windows.

Microsoft Download Center, `www.microsoft.com/downloads/search.asp?`, takes you to free downloadable enhancements for Windows 98.

Windows Users Group Network, `www.wugnet.com/win98`, has a wealth of unofficial, practical information about using Windows 98.

Next time you're on the Internet, don't forget to drop by `www.cliffsnotes.com`. We created an online Resource Center that you can use today, tomorrow, and beyond.

Magazines and Other Media

PC World, at your local newsstand, shows you the latest news and tips for your PC and how changes in the software industry affect it. Sample its wares at `www.1pcworld.com`.

Send Us Your Favorite Tips

In your quest for knowledge, have you ever experienced that sublime moment when you figure out a trick that saves time or trouble? Perhaps you realized you were taking ten steps to accomplish something that could take two. Or you found a little-known workaround that achieved great results. If you've discovered a useful tip that helped you use Windows 98 more effectively, and you'd like to share it, the CliffsNotes staff would love to hear from you. Go to our Web site at `www.cliffsnotes.com` and click the Talk to Us button. If we select your tip, we may publish it as part of CliffsNotes Daily, our exciting, free e-mail newsletter. To find out more or to subscribe to a newsletter, go to `www.cliffsnotes.com` on the Web.

INDEX

COMING SOON FROM CLIFFSNOTES

Online Shopping

HTML

Choosing a PC

Beginning Programming

Careers

Windows 98 Home Networking

eBay Online Auctions

PC Upgrade and Repair

Business

Microsoft Word 2000

Microsoft PowerPoint 2000

Finance

Microsoft Outlook 2000

Digital Photography

Palm Computing

Investing

Windows 2000

Online Research

IDG BOOKS
WORLDWIDE

COMING SOON FROM CLIFFSNOTES
Buying and Selling on eBay

Have you ever experienced the thrill of finding an incredible bargain at a specialty store or been amazed at what people are willing to pay for things that you might toss in the garbage? If so, then you'll want to learn about eBay — the hottest auction site on the Internet. And CliffsNotes *Buying and Selling on eBay* is the shortest distance to eBay proficiency. You'll learn how to:

■ Find what you're looking for, from antique toys to classic cars

■ Watch the auctions strategically and place bids at the right time

■ Sell items online at the eBay site

■ Make the items you sell attractive to prospective bidders

■ Protect yourself from fraud

Here's an example of how the step-by-step CliffsNotes learning process simplifies placing a bid at eBay:

1. Scroll to the Web page form that is located at the bottom of the page on which the auction item itself is presented.

2. Enter your registered eBay username and password and enter the amount you want to bid. A Web page appears that lets you review your bid before you actually submit it to eBay. After you're satisfied with your bid, click the Place Bid button.

3. Click the Back button on your browser until you return to the auction listing page. Then choose View⇨Reload (Netscape Navigator) or View⇨Refresh (Microsoft Internet Explorer) to reload the Web page information. Your new high bid appears on the Web page, and your name appears as the high bidder.